Human Resources for School Leaders

"In *Human Resources: A Practical Guide for School Leaders*, authors Fowler and Davis provide what is perhaps the most comprehensive book to date on human resources processes at both the district and building levels within the TK-12 educational setting. I highly recommend this text for all aspiring and practicing school leaders."

—**Dr. Sarah M. Jouganatos** (Program Coordinator & Associate Professor, Educational Leadership & Policy Studies, California State University, Sacramento)

"Davis and Fowler have written the comprehensive book on developing and retaining the best teachers for our schools. *Human Resources: A Practical Guide for School Leaders* is practical, research based, and innovative in its approach; a must read."

—**Dr. Chris Colwell** (Associate Professor & Chair, Department of Education, Stetson University)

"*Human Resources: A Practical Guide for School Leaders* serves as a realistic and reflective tool for leaders in the field of education at all levels. The use of relevant case studies and reflective questions allows the reader to deeply reflect upon and refine current organizational practices. I strongly encourage those who wish to enter the field of educational leadership, as well as current building and district level leaders, to embark on the human resources journey with the authors."

—**Dr. Robert Hill** (Superintendent, Springfield City School District)

"Doug and Denver really get human development. The book makes clear that the investment in people is worth it. The practical approach to human development is truly a practical approach as outlined throughout the book. The ideas and strategies focused on the building level are timeline and tangible. Readers will also appreciate the follow-up resources and community leveraged around the book at #HRforLeaders."

—**Dr. Trent Grundmeyer** (Associate Professor, Educational Leadership, Drake University)

"The *Human Resources: A Practical Guide for School Leaders* is a text that must be adopted by every principal preparation program. While most human resources texts are written from a district-level perspective, the reality is that many of the recruiting, hiring, inducting, assessing, and developing of teachers is done by principals at the building level. This text infuses 12 excellent case reflections, which will be vitally important in the preparation of the next generation of principals leading our schools!"

—**Dr. David De Jong** (Assistant Professor, Educational Leadership, University of South Dakota)

"A sensible, analytical, and technical look at the processes behind human resource development in education, this work provides a great foundation for the development of people in the people industry."

—**Mr. Kenneth J. Hopkins Jr.** (Assistant Principal [former *Assistant Principal of the Year* in the state of Rhode Island], Smithfield High School)

"*Human Resources: A Practical Guide for School Leaders* gets at the very heart of best practices and what is best for students as it applies to human resources practices at both the building and district levels within the PreK-12 educational setting. I highly recommend this text for aspiring and practicing school leaders across our nation and around the globe."

—**Dr. Patrick A. Bennett** (Dean, School of Education, Franklin University)

"Davis and Fowler's work paves a clear path for the school leader as the defacto human resources coordinator of the learning community. This book takes readers through recruiting, mentoring and ultimately developing future school leaders. The real world scenarios outlined here coupled with the introspective questions at each chapter's end have deeply shifted my understanding of HRD in schools."

—**Walter Brown** (Co-founder of New York City Department of Education's #EDxEDNYC Annual Conference and current Assistant Principal of Hudson High School of Learning Technologies in New York City)

Human Resources for School Leaders

11 Steps to Utilizing HR to Improve Student Learning

Douglas R. Davis and Denver J. Fowler

ROWMAN & LITTLEFIELD
Lanham • Boulder • New York • London

Published by Rowman & Littlefield
An imprint of The Rowman & Littlefield Publishing Group, Inc.
4501 Forbes Boulevard, Suite 200, Lanham, Maryland 20706
www.rowman.com

6 Tinworth Street, London SE11 5AL, United Kingdom

Copyright © 2020 by Denver J. Fowler and Douglas R. Davis

All rights reserved. No part of this book may be reproduced in any form or by any electronic or mechanical means, including information storage and retrieval systems, without written permission from the publisher, except by a reviewer who may quote passages in a review.

British Library Cataloguing in Publication Information Available

Library of Congress Cataloging-in-Publication Data Available

ISBN 978-1-4758-3710-0 (cloth)
ISBN 978-1-4758-3711-7 (pbk.)
ISBN 978-1-4758-3712-4 (electronic)

Dedication by Dr. Douglas R. Davis

This book is dedicated to my wife, colleague as a professor in educational leadership at the University of Mississippi, and number one supporter, Dr. Jill Cabrera Davis. Thank you for your continuous encouragement, conversations, and love. It is an honor to share with my spouse and partner a commitment to improving public education in our community, state, and nation. It is a blessing to share one of the primary purposes we choose in our lives. You bring joy to our days and meaning to what we do. My appreciation is endless.

To my parents, William E. (Bud) Davis and Pollyanne Davis who taught me about leadership through a lifetime of positive examples. Dad, you showed by your example your repeated claim that, "When there is true leadership and the job is well done, the people say we did it ourselves." You both showed me leaders have compassion and care about all people, leaders serve with humility and place the good of the organization above their own interests, leaders never shut their doors and always listen, and leaders work with people and not over them. I believe the content of this book reflects the values you continue to exemplify as you enter into your ninety-second year of life and sixty-ninth year of marriage. You remain my model for living a life of grace, passion, and service to others.

To my graduate school and professional mentors, Dr. Al McWilliams, Dr. Ben Baez, Dr. Chad Ellett, Dr. Spencer Maxcy, and Dr. Richard Fossey. You are instrumental in my advanced education, which guides my work today. You taught me how to be a scholar and a professor. You modeled being a student-centered professor and I have always tried to replicate your dedication and service to students. You believed in me and gave me the inspiration and confidence to pursue a career in the academy. To you, and all the many others who have supported my journey in education, I am deeply grateful.

Finally, I would like to thank Emily Wells for careful editing of this work. Your time and attention is deeply appreciated.

Dedication by Dr. Denver J. Fowler

I would like to dedicate this book to my wife and best friend, Anna Caroline Fowler. Thank you for your unconditional love, unwavering support, and consistently sound advice. "God blessed the broken road that led me straight to you."

To my daughter, Haley Jade Fowler, and my two sons, Beckett Daniel Fowler and Teagan Robertson Fowler. May you forever remain curious and always chase your wildest dreams, whatever they may be.

To my mother, Cathie Jane Fowler, a single parent who worked two and three jobs her entire life to raise my brother and I. Thank you for all of the sacrifices that you made for us. They did not go unnoticed. Thank you for always telling me that I can accomplish anything, to always chase my dreams, and to always focus on what I have, versus what I do not.

To my brother, Levi Hunter Fowler, we've been through it all together, and we still rose from the ashes. Glory be to God!

I would also like to dedicate this book to my late grandpa, 1st Lt. Francis 'Fritz' Moran, an Indian motorcycle dirt track racer and Tank Commander in World War II, fighting in two major campaigns, The Battle of the Bulge and Normandy, later receiving the Purple Heart. My late grandma, Helen Moran, who held a family together years before they began to diagnose our soldiers with post-traumatic stress disorder.

My late grandpa, George Lee Fowler, who coal mined his entire life in the coal mines of West Virginia, before eventually dying of black lung disease. My late grandma, Mary Katherine Fowler, who was a *Rosie the Riveter* during World War II and successfully raised 13 children on miner's pay.

To my late uncle, Chris Fowler, a Veteran who worked construction and rode Harleys his entire life. You were there for me so many times to offer sound advice. Thank you.

To my late uncle, Patrick Moran, a Vietnam Veteran who never really came home from the Vietnam War.

To all the teachers, coaches, professors, colleagues, friends and family members who have consistently "nudged my boat" over the years. Thank you for believing in me.

Finally, to all the individuals working in the education setting. We have the most important job in the world. Don't ever forget that. Our children's hopes and dreams start and end with you each and every day. Teach them to dream big and be great!

God, Family, Academics, Athletics, the Arts.

Contents

List of Tables   xi
List of Case Reflections   xiii
Foreword by Dr. David De Jong   xv
Preface   xvii

SECTION I: FOUNDATIONS OF HUMAN RESOURCE DEVELOPMENT   **1**

1   Leadership and Human Resources Development and the Role of Human Resources in Educational Organizations   3
2   Economic Theory and Developing Human Resources   19
3   Strategic Planning for Developing Human Resources   33
4   Utilizing Technology with Human Resources   46

SECTION II: HIRING AND RETAINING TEACHERS   **55**

5   Successfully Recruiting and Hiring Instructional Personnel   57
6   New Teacher Induction and Mentoring   73

SECTION III: DEVELOPING TEACHER QUALITY   **81**

7   The Role of Assessing Teaching and Learning in Promoting Organizational Change   83

8	Methods and Value of Assessing Teaching and Learning Processes for Professional Growth	92
9	Leadership and Developing Human Resources in Educational Organizations through Professional Development	104

SECTION IV: MISCELLANEOUS 113

10	Dealing with Marginal Teachers	115
11	Recent Innovations and Human Resources	124

Afterword by Dr. Christopher Colwell	133
References	135
About the Authors	141
Index	144

List of Tables

3.1	Mississippi National Assessment of Educational Progress (NAEP) Scale Score and National Rank Changes 2013–2019	38
3.2	JPS Strategic Plan—Ten Targeted Outcomes	42
3.3	JPS Implementation Plan Example: Commitment #1: A Strong Start	44
5.1	Advertising Options for Instructional Positions in a School	60
5.2	Prescreening Applicants for Instructional Positions	65
5.3	Example Scaled Total Score for Instructional Applicant	67
7.1	A Comparison of Professional Development and Staff Development in Schools	86
8.1	Game Statistics	93
9.1	Planning a Professional Development Program	105
9.2	Commonly Available Data Types Used in Schools and Options for Disaggregation	107
9.3	Data Examples for Gap Analyses and Goal Determination	108

List of Case Reflections

Case Reflection 1	"Wish You Were Here" or "Wasting Away Again in Margaritaville"	12
Case Reflection 2	"Maggie Sells Her Speech Services to a New Buyer"	24
Case Reflection 3	Strategic Planning Audit	44
Case Reflection 4	"Look Out Honey, Cause I'm Using Technology"	53
Case Reflection 5	Post-Interview Surprise	70
Case Reflection 6	New Teacher Induction	73
Case Reflection 7	The Knight in Shining Armor	89
Case Reflection 8	A Football Analogy	93
Case Reflection 9	Review of the Link between Assessed Needs, Organizational Goals, and Professional Development Processes	111
Case Reflection 10	The Mad Coach	121
Case Reflection 11	"I Want Money, That's What I Want . . ."	127

Foreword by Dr. David De Jong

It was the end of my first year as a principal, and I remember feeling overwhelmed the moment I learned that one of the best teachers in my school was going to retire at the end of the year. I knew it was my responsibility to find an awesome teacher to replace the retiring teacher, but I had more questions than answers. Where should we advertise? Which technology should I use to get the word out about our open position? Which questions should we use when we interview? Once a teacher is hired, how do I assign that teacher a mentor teacher? What should be on the agenda for the new teacher orientation? What should I do during the teacher's first year in the school? Again, I had more questions than answers. As I read *Human Resources for School Leaders* by Davis and Fowler, one thought continually came to my head. I wish I had a time machine so I could go back to my first year as a principal and follow the practical advice in this book.

I have now had the privilege of leading over one hundred searches for positions ranging from preschool teachers to tenure-track faculty in higher education, and I can affirm that the practical advice from Davis and Fowler is exactly what school leaders need as they aspire to play an important role in the human resource process in their school and their district. I also teach human resources at the graduate school level and plan on adopting this book once it is published.

The *Human Resources for School Leaders* is easy to read and uses economics as the framework. Some of the practical advice explained in this book includes:

- Tips for using Instagram, Twitter, Facebook, Hootsuite, and other cutting-edge technologies in the human resource process;

- Being intentional and deliberate about how one introduces a new employee on staff;
- Understanding that professional development time for teachers has a cost, where a one-hour faculty meeting may cost thousands of dollars in salaries and benefits;
- Dealing with incompetent teachers; and
- An entire chapter devoted to innovations in human resources, which includes perks for teachers such as childcare, gym memberships, housing, paid sabbaticals, and the like.

The *Human Resources for School Leaders* is a book that must be adopted by every principal preparation program. While most human resources texts are written from a district-level perspective, the reality is that many of the recruiting, hiring, inducting, assessing, and developing of teachers is done by principals at the building level. This text infuses eleven excellent case reflections, which will be vitally important in the preparation of the next generation of principals leading our schools!

Dr. David De Jong
University of South Dakota

Preface

Human Resources for School Leaders is designed to support and sustain improved student learning in schools. In addition, the book presents a comprehensive approach for improving teacher quality within schools. Across the nation, there is evidence (Carver-Thomas & Darling-Hammond, 2017; Carver-Thomas & Darling-Hammond, 2019; Sutcher, Darling-Hammond, & Carver-Thomas, 2016) that the teaching profession is in a crisis with increasing teacher turnover and growing teacher shortages nationwide.

According to Carver-Thomas and Darling-Hammond (2017), annual turnover rates for teachers vary from 10.3 percent in the Northeast to 16.7 percent in the South. For schools serving more low-income students (i.e., Title I), turnover rates are an additional 50 percent higher for all teachers, and up to 80 percent higher for math and science teachers. Unfortunately, schools, especially schools serving students in poverty, are finding it difficult to hire qualified teachers. Sutcher, Darling-Hammond, and Carver-Thomas (2016) estimate the 2018 teacher shortage in the United States to be 112,000. Further, the model used in this research conducted at the Learning Policy Institute (Sutcher et al., 2017) predicts the teacher shortage will continue at a high level of over 100,000 per year until at least 2025. It is clear that the difficult challenge for school leaders to hire and retain teachers with the knowledge and skills to meet the needs of students is growing. The words of a school leader (Young, 2017) focus the meaning of these national data for practicing school-level administrators:

> We are in such a mess with needing teachers that I think we have to consider placement of staff in a way that students will not go their entire educational career without ever having a highly qualified teacher. This became obvious to me when the district leadership team was discussing an elementary school who

has a teacher qualified to teach 7th-8th grade English while we have two TFAs and one long term substitute in the 7th and 8th grade ELA classrooms. Additionally, recent observations in our district's schools revealed that every other classroom is manned by a long-termed substitute or short-term sub who has no education background. We are in a state of emergency and nobody is ringing the alarm.

Research (Engel, Jacob, & Curran, 2014) suggests this problem is most severe in schools performing poorly.

Poor-performing schools, often serving a high-poverty population, are finding it increasingly difficult to recruit, hire, develop, and retain a high-quality professional teaching force. Regardless, additional evidence (Jehangir, Glas, van den Berg, 2015; von Stumm, 2017; von Stumm & Plomin, 2015; von Stumm, Deary, & Hagger-Johnson, 2013) shows that even high-performing schools struggle to meet the needs of all students, and achievement gaps based on the economic status of students are essentially universal in the American education system.

A key variable in closing achievement gaps in schools and across districts is teacher quality (Hanushek, 2011), or the capacity of teachers to provide effective instruction, and this book posits that leadership in the areas of human resources, both systemic and cultural, is essential for increasing the instructional capacity of teachers. This book views human resource development (HRD) as integrated into all aspects of school leadership. Developing human resources is not a separate area of practice in need of isolated attention and focus nor are other areas of leadership independent from HRD. The emphasis is on increasing instructional capacity. While there are other aspects of HRD relevant to administrative practice, the emphasis here is the development of teachers in order to target the essential mandate of school leaders to improve instruction. Thus, the book covers the systemic elements (policies, organizational structures, and operational practices) of recruiting, hiring, inducting, assessing, developing, and retaining effective teachers; and the organizational cultural characteristics to support these systems.

To understand the importance of an uncommon HRD emphasis on organizational culture, consider a school with a desire to provide a positive first year experience for new teachers. In order to provide the positive experience, the school seeks to develop a work environment in which new teachers are glad to launch into a teaching profession and look forward to coming to work each day. The goal is to create an environment to both retain and develop the skills of new teachers. In order to meet this goal, the school must not only have strong systems in place to support new teachers, but it must also have a culture characterized by an authentic professional learning community (PLC) supportive of the social, professional, and collaborative needs of new teachers. This is not a simple task. Effective HRD practices are expensive, time-consuming, and require high levels of individual and organizational commitment. In addition, the essence of this area of administrative practice is economic. The organization, typically a government entity (school district) or a private interest (private school), is paying an individual teacher to provide a professional service. The fundamental transactional nature of the relationship between schools and teachers is why economics is one of the theoretical frameworks used in this book. The economic frame does not diminish the fundamental human nature of teaching and learning; rather, it emphasizes the value of education and the economic worth of individuals skilled in the task of educating.

Quality teaching is of great value, and a proper accounting of this value supports the need, development, and adequate and fair compensation of quality teachers. While HRD is an expensive and time-consuming commitment, it is a critical investment needed to improve schools. It is also an efficient investment because the successful recruiting, hiring, inducting, assessing, developing, and retaining teachers lowers the need for these investments in the future.

Human Resources for School Leaders presents a new and unique perspective on HRD in schools in several ways. First, the focus is on the building level. While HRD functions are often housed in the central office, especially in large districts, key decisions relating to recruiting, hiring, inducting, assessing, and developing teachers belong within the schoolhouse doors. While districts will typically set guidelines, establish timelines and procedures, ensure legal compliance, and provide schools with administrative support and resources, personnel in schools are best situated to make better decisions based on the needs of each individual school. In support of building-level decisions, the second unique feature of this book is the focus on technology, especially social media, Apps, streaming, and communication, to improve the success and efficiency of HRD processes.

The use of technology supports the third area of focus that is utilizing data-based decisions in all HRD processes. Specifically, an emphasis is placed on assessment of teaching and learning in all roles of HRD, including identifying instructional needs to target recruiting, assessing applicants, assessing the needs of new teachers, driving professional growth, and improving marginal teachers. A fourth focus is developing learning organizations and engaging in cycles of continuous improvement. Specifically, an emphasis is placed on continually monitoring, evaluating, and revising HRD practices in a plan, do, check, and act cycle. Finally, the text is consistent with and is designed to support the professional learning communities and sustained school change.

Given positive change in a school requires increased instructional capacity, there are two mechanisms to increase capacity. First, schools may replace a departing teacher with a new teacher having a higher level of professional knowledge and skill. Or, schools may increase the professional knowledge and skills of current teachers.

With these five new and unique areas of focus, the value of *Human Resources for School Leaders* is organized around *11 steps to Utilizing HR to Improve Student Learning:*

1. *Embedding HRD in all areas of school-level administrative practice* (Chapter One).
2. *Cost effective and efficient HRD* (Chapter Two).
3. *Planning for effective HRD* (Chapter Three).
4. *Using technology to support HRD* (Chapter Four).
5. *Recruiting teachers* (Chapter Five).
6. *Hiring teachers* (Chapter Five).
7. *Inducting new teachers* (Chapter Six).
8. *Assessing teaching and learning* (Chapters Seven-Nine).
9. *Targeted professional growth* (Chapters Seven-Nine).
10. *Dealing with marginal teachers* (Chapter Ten).
11. *Innovations to attract, support, and retain teachers* (Chapter Eleven).

Section I

FOUNDATIONS OF HUMAN RESOURCE DEVELOPMENT

Chapter 1

Leadership and Human Resources Development and the Role of Human Resources in Educational Organizations

INTRODUCTION

The purpose of this introductory chapter is to situate human resource development (HRD) within building-level educational leadership practice. Three primary needs of school leadership establish a set of common themes for the book. These three themes overlap, relate, and depend on one another. *Human Resources for School Leaders* is, first, a book about school leadership. Leadership is the purposeful cultivation of cooperative human relationships for the purpose of achieving socially determined and defined goals through the organized social systems called organizations.

This definition does not constrain leadership to administrators. Rather, the constructs of leadership density and leadership capacity in an organization (Smith & Ellett, 2000) are centered throughout this book. Leadership density is a measure of leadership in an organization based on a hypothetical average of leadership productivity spread across all members promoting the accomplishment of organizational goals. Schools with high leadership density have a higher level of professional educators engaged in leadership activities than schools with low leadership density.

Smith and Ellett (2000) found a significant relationship between leadership density and school performance. The data suggest high leadership density schools characterized by shared collective responsibility for the success of all students. Consistent with this model, leadership in a school is both a characteristic of individuals and a collective characteristic of the organization. Individuals and organizations have leadership potential and capacity. As result, the content of this book is relevant and useful to all professional educators committed to the success of students.

To understand the role of HRD in a school, three leadership themes are presented:

1. Recognizing of leadership and the paradox of HRD in a school;
2. The organizational of a school and HRD; and
3. The teaching and learning process and HRD.

Success in each theme requires collegial, cooperative, and positive relationships between professional educators—all require leadership. In order to link leadership theory and practice to HRD, this chapter describes and explains these three themes, discusses some of the leadership challenges and opportunities of HRD, and concludes with a discussion on the meaning and value of theory.

THE PARADOX OF HRD

The paradox of managing HRD results from the organizational role of school principals serving both teachers and the school system. The profession of public education is characterized by two constituencies striving for increased influence under constant tension, and a school-based administrator practices as a point of mediation between these competing interests. While these two groups, the public citizenry and the profession of teaching, share a common goal of providing effective education to all children, organizational structures of the U.S. public education systems often create a dynamic of contending interests between these two groups.

The first constituency resides from citizens in accordance with the American democratic system of government. Public schools are financed by taxpayer money and operated through publicly controlled bureaucracies. At the top of the hierarchy are the departments of education in each state. Since the passage of the No Child Left Behind Act (2002) (NCLB), the federal government is playing a greater role in school policy and governance. Nonetheless, under the Tenth Amendment of the U.S. Constitution (the establishment clause), states are vested with the responsibility to develop and maintain systems to provide for the education of children. According to the Tenth Amendment, powers not directly granted to the federal government are reserved to the states.

Because a system of public education is not included in the U.S. Constitution, rights to and requirements for providing public educations exist only in the constitutions of the individual states. While states typically set broad policies for the operations of schools, establish financial guidelines for taxation and funding, and license professional educators, they rarely directly manage schools. To provide for local governance of schools, states typically grant *charters* (usually a county or some unified distinction based on local municipal structure) to special local agencies (districts) to construct, maintain, and operate public schools. Representative school board members who are elected by voters or appointed through a political process seek to maximize the efficient use of public education dollars through policy-based systematic processes.

The local role of governance in education is the foundation of the public school system in the United States, however, it frequently manifests in a dual political agenda of local needs. The first agenda is to improve performance (i.e., increase test scores and improve relative performance compared to other schools, districts, states, and even nations) and the second agenda is to reduce costs and lower taxes. Thus, school boards have a vested responsibility of overseeing a public bureaucracy established to educate children at a high level with minimum cost. The use of a public bureaucracy to operate schools results in a system led by school boards who *appoint top managers*, *make policy* (organizational, procedural, and regulatory), and *allocate resources*. From the position of school board members or other top elected officials, the superintendent in some cases, the mechanisms for improvement are primarily systemic, structural, and formal.

These characteristics of school organizations, defined as open-systems (transparent organizations permeable to public feedback and influence), are described by Hoy and Miskel (2013) as the policies, procedures, job descriptions, and guidelines found in organization systems which provide goods and services. The nature of this structure in public education is a top-down hierarchical system, which is controlled by voters, and created to provide a public service for the benefit of all citizens. Authority and control of the system is intentionally centered at the top of the hierarchy with school boards, and authority in the system flows down through the central office to the school buildings, which ultimately comes down to the individual teachers in the classroom. Thus, a building-level principal and all professional personnel working in public schools work for the citizens of his or her district.

The opposing constituency of influence is the teaching profession. The profession of teaching is historically, and remains today, a field striving for professional recognition and autonomy. There are many characteristics of public school teaching described in classical descriptions of a profession (Švarc, 2016), including advanced education, creative thinking, job commitment, learning opportunities, and access to networks of experts. Regardless, the most defining characteristics of a profession are the control of production and the autonomy of practice, and these are rare in the K-12 teaching profession. Thus, teaching is essentially a *quasi-profession* because teachers do not have the autonomy and control of practice that is common in other professional fields. Elmore (2016) makes this point in manner worthy of quoting:

> Professions do indeed have practices that they expect their members to use and they evaluate themselves according to how well those practices work. But

in real professions, of which education is not one, those practices come at the end of a long causal chain of learning and cultural socialization that creates foundational knowledge, dispositions toward the acquisition of new knowledge, and formal and informal institutions that stand apart from the workplace and that reinforce the culture that produces the practice. Real professions select their members based on mastery of knowledge, not based on bureaucratic and institutional procedures. Educators, because of the weakness of professional culture and autonomy, tend to treat "best practices" as tips and tricks that can be readily assimilated by reading the right books, or hiring the right consultants, rather than by investing seriously in developing the cultural and institutional infrastructures of professional practice. (p. 531)

Historically, teachers as a professional body have sought to increase control of their own professional practice (Goldstein, 2014). Goldstein argues that many of the struggles of contemporary teachers echo past challenges; nonetheless, because teachers are providers of teaching and learning services, they remain a powerful force, and little gets done in an educational organization without the support of teachers. A school-based administrator practices in the middle of these two broad and often conflicting constituencies.

It is a rare administrator who survives the wrath of groups of tax-paying public or of united teachers. When it comes to HRD, the principal is expected to hire, supervise, develop, and evaluate instructional personnel. In addition, principals must implement and enforce system policies, procedures, and initiatives. Regardless of these factors, school leaders are expected to support and meet the professional needs of teachers as a collaborative colleague—one of the strongest needs being professional autonomy of practice. Success or failure in these areas impacts the organizational culture and the achievement of organizational goals. Effective school leaders are able to balance these two constituencies within a shared commitment to a single vision. In balancing the structural bureaucracy with the profession of teaching, the key to success is a strong and a positive organizational culture.

STRENGTHENING THE ORGANIZATIONAL CULTURE IN A SCHOOL THROUGH HRD

There are many definitions of school culture. As a guide for effective HRD, the Glossary of Education Reform's (n.d.) provides a thorough and useful description of school culture:

The term school culture generally refers to the beliefs, perceptions, relationships, attitudes, and written and unwritten rules that shape and influence every aspect of how a school functions, but the term also encompasses more concrete issues such as the physical and emotional safety of students, the orderliness of classrooms and public spaces, or the degree to which a school embraces and celebrates racial, ethnic, linguistic, or cultural diversity.

A simple definition of school culture is the norms, values, and beliefs of members in an organization. Culture is the shared meaning in a group of "who we are, what we believe, what we do, and how we do it." An understanding of the importance of organizational culture is essential to effective HRD. There is much evidence a strong and positive culture is a characteristic of high-performing schools (Elmore, 2000; Fullan, 2001; Fullan, 2015; Fullan, Hill, & Crevola, 2006).

At the dawn of the twentieth century, during the progressive era, an emphasis on the role of organizational culture and level of performance was championed by Mary Parker Follett (Follett, 1919; Stout & Love, 2015; Whipps, 2014). The nature of Follett's cultural orientation through what she called interpenetration is explained in *Integrative Process: Follettian Thinking from Ontology to Administration* (Stout & Love, 2015). Outcomes in well-functioning groups emerge from a synthesis of shared understanding, rather than system rules based on hierarchy and compromise. When members of a group is characterized by a culture of interpenetration, the members are able to achieve different perspectives on issues and reach consensus. Follett used the term interpenetration to describe a process of group discussions to achieve a common understanding of organizational practice.

Later in the early twentieth century, another progressive thinker, John Dewey, grounded learning in culture. Dewey was a philosopher in the American pragmatic tradition and his views of education emphasized the close relationship between education and experience (Dewey, 1919; Dewey, 1938; Heilbronn, 2017). For Dewey, education is a result of experience through social interaction in a contextual culture. According to Heilbronn's (2017) understanding of Dewey:

> Culture can be taken as a useful term to encapsulate the complex inter-relationship between material and symbolic resources that develop and maintain habits, and it is with the shaping of habits that I am particularly concerned. . . , the habit shaped by school, school encounters with others, the curriculum and the "being" constructed in associated living. (p. 93)

Dewey clearly understood education as a behavioral and social activity, and in response he focused on context and meaning. From Dewey's perspective, the culture, or the nature of human behavior and interaction in a group, is education.

The interest in culture and how it affects organizational effectiveness was emphasized in the work of Edwards Deming (1986) following World War II.

During the war, Deming served on the five-member Emergency Technical Committee and advised wartime production managers on applied statistical methods and was credited with many innovations leading to increased productivity. After World War II, Deming spent many years in Japan and was involved with the dramatic development of Japan into a global economic power. It was not until the 1980s and the release of *Out of the Crisis* (1986) that Deming became widely known in the United States. Deming rejected assumptions based on finding the best way to accomplish an organizational task, and he embraced "continuous quality improvements."

He recognized that optimal methods could never be stable in ever-changing internal and external contexts. Even though he never used the term, Deming is best known for developing the principles of total quality management (TQM). Deming's model of improving organizational performance is often misunderstood and misapplied with the single focus on using data to inform decisions at all levels of an organization. This was certainly an area of focus for Deming; however, this single focus overlooks his emphasis on the importance of human relationships to quality. Knouse et al. (2009) describe the cultural orientation of Deming's thinking as follows: "Employee empowerment encourages active employee participation in the organization and implies a basic level of trust between management and employees in order to share ideas for continuous improvement" (p. 455). Near the end of his life, Deming's focus on decision making at the production level, most were related to the culture of an organization:

1. Create constancy of purpose toward improvement of product and service.
2. Adopt the new philosophy.
3. Cease dependence on inspection to achieve quality.
4. End the practice of awarding business on the basis of price tag.
5. Improve constantly and forever the system.
6. Institute training on the job.
7. Institute leadership.
8. Drive out fear.
9. Break down barriers between departments.
10. Eliminate slogans and exhortations.
11. Eliminate quotas.
12. Remove barriers that rob people of pride of workmanship.
13. Institute education and self-improvement.
14. Put everybody to work to accomplish the transformation.

Constancy of purpose, philosophy, leadership, driving out fear, breaking down barriers, and involving everybody are all consistent with the descriptions of culture used in this book.

Research in education began to focus on the role of culture in school performance during the 1960s and, during the 1980s, mounting evidence began to emerge directly linking organizational culture to effective schools. This analysis remains one of the most influential strands of educational research in the field. This body of research is collectively known as the *effective schools research* (Edmonds, 1981, 1982; Hallinger & Murphy, 1986; Teddlie, Kirby, & Stringfield, 1989). The influence of the effective schools research is evident on current standards for leadership preparation: National Educational Leadership Preparation (NELP) standards; and practice: Professional Standards for Educational Leadership (PSEL). Effective schools research is inductive. It starts with results (effects) and searches for causes (or from specific cases to general conclusions). Typically, effective schools research identifies a large group of schools with similar demographic characteristics (level, context, and socioeconomic status [SES] variables). Based on output measures (test scores), the highest- and lowest-performing schools are identified—usually the top and bottom 2 to 3 percent within a group of schools with similar characteristics. Once the target schools are selected, researchers conduct extensive qualitative and quantitative research investigations on conditions in the highest- and lowest-performing schools. A consistent outcome from this large and diverse body of research is that effective schools have strong organizational cultures. The studies suggest that cultural variables, specifically a strong sense of shared vision and instructional focus, are central to effective schools (Goddard et al., 2015; Hallinger & Heck, 1998; Kurland, Peretz, & Hertz-Lazarowitz, 2010).

Today, the importance of culture is championed by leading scholars in the field of education. In education, "shared-vision" is a catch-all term for a strong culture. There is a research-based connection between "vision" and its use as the focus of PSEL Standard 1. Fullan, Hill, and Crevola (2006) argue that the key to student success is personalization and precision. Simple in concept and difficult in implementation, personalization and precision require a response to the unique needs of each student at the proper time. According to Fullan (2016), personalization and precision only occur in schools where every teacher works with other teachers to improve every day. Fullan makes it explicitly clear that standards and structural changes are not enough to change a school—a cultural shift is required.

The social scientific understanding of the relationship between the organizational culture of a school and the performance of the school, a topic covered throughout the book, is explained well by Richard Elmore (2016). Elmore warns of an oversimplified understanding of the complexity of organizational culture and change and is suspect of prescriptive policy recommendations. The issue is the bureaucratic organizations common in schools; "Trying to graft a professional culture onto an essentially bureaucratic, heavily institutionalized culture is a thankless task. The things that are easily 'scaleable' in this environment are the things that require the least depth of preparation and practice" (Elmore, 2016, p. 531). Elmore issues a challenge to educators to understand the limits from a packaged solution to complex problems and he logically suggests that the characteristics of the organization matter more than the policies being implemented. This challenge is embraced throughout this text.

The book emphasizes how all leaders in an organization relate to the people performing the work; in other words, how people working in a school relate to each other as professionals. It is imperative to rethink the nature of how schools are structured and operate in order to overcome the reality that "our conceptions of what is possible are too often constrained by our beliefs about what is feasible and practical in an archaic set of institutions" (Elmore, 2016, p. 537). Along with culture, however, the other critical and related element of successful schools is the teaching and learning process.

A SCHOOL WHERE PEOPLE WANT TO BE IS AN INDICATION OF A STRONG POSITIVE CULTURE (DOUGLAS DAVIS)

Here is a practical method of identifying a strong culture. Several years ago, I was asked to conduct a comprehensive assessment of the lowest-performing elementary school in a large metropolitan area in the southeast. The purpose of this activity was to assess the problems in the school and make recommendations for change and improvement. A team of three graduate students and I went into the school and interviewed twenty teachers and all three administrators (principal, assistant principal [AP], and the instructional support teacher), observed thirty-two class sessions, surveyed all the teachers and 120 students, and held focus groups with parents and community members. While the situation was complex and we found many strengths and weaknesses, one result struck us as particularly poignant: the data showed that across the board, from all three administrators, the teachers, the students, and the parents, no one wanted to be at the school. The principal (in his first year and the school's ninth principal in eleven years) told me he could not wait to get out of there. Several parents related they were planning to move their children into a different school. Survey results suggested a school rife with conflict, dissolution, and dissent. In short, the culture in this school was toxic and its performance reflected this. From this study, we concluded that a good indicator of a strong and positive organizational culture is an organization where individuals want to be involved. A school with a strong culture is a school where people want to be.

IMPROVING TEACHING AND LEARNING PROCESSES THROUGH HRD

Universal truths are rare in the social sciences, especially in education. Regardless, here is one: classroom teaching and learning is a behavioral process and as a result, teaching and learning (and student achievement) will not improve unless teachers change their own behaviors in the classroom. Thus, if a leader wishes to improve teaching and learning in a school, he or she must influence a sustainable change in the professional behavior and practice of adults. The purpose of HRD in a service-providing organization is to bring the most qualified individuals into the group and continuously develop each person's productive capacity to provide a professional service. Thus, leadership, both individual and collective, requires influencing and changing the behavior of individuals in a group. The teaching and learning process in each classroom in a school is the essence of school improvement and organizational success. More than any other factor, the teacher is the key variable in the quality of the teaching and learning process (Printy & Marks, 2006; Marzano, Waters, & McNulty, 2005).

Effective HRD leadership is the key to making a positive impact on getting the best quality teachers into classrooms and maximizing the professional potential of these individuals. The key components of this book are focused on achieving this goal. Successful administrative and teacher leadership in each of these areas is critical to supporting and sustaining improved teaching and learning in a school:

- Successful recruiting increases the quality and diversity of an applicant pool for a position.
- Successful hiring processes support the assessment and selection of the most qualified person available who is a good "fit" within the organizational culture.
- Successful induction allows for the assessment of the needs of new teachers and for the organization to meet the needs of new instructional personnel, increase teacher retention, and improve morale.
- Successful assessment of classroom teaching and learning allows teachers to target strengths and weaknesses and allows targeted professional growth to improve instructional practices.
- Successful professional growth promotes and builds collaboration and team work and improves teaching and learning through increased collective teacher efficacy (Ross & Gray, 2006).

In summary, while there are many organizational lenses through which a school leader may operate to improve teaching and learning, the three themes of understanding and managing the paradox of HRD, strengthening organizational culture, and improving teaching and learning through HRD make a compelling case for centering HRD as a framework for improved performance. Thus, the goal of this book is to develop knowledge and skills through the simple, yet difficult to actualize, concept of developing successful HRD practices and processes to mediate tensions between professional norms and bureaucratic structures in a school, strengthen organizational culture, and improve teaching and learning. The next sections examine existing challenges and opportunities of utilizing an HRD approach to improving schools.

Case Reflection 1

"Wish You Were Here" or "Wasting Away Again in Margaritaville"

Not a speck of dust has settled on your new award as the "Principal of the Year" in Hi-Hope County. Certainly, you have reason to be proud. Test scores at Onthetop Middle School have risen for the sixth consecutive year since you assumed leadership of the school. Unfortunately, the big award is going to make it that much harder to explain to your spouse and children why, once again, you will not be joining them next week for the annual family vacation to Mexico. For a brief moment you mistake the taste in your mouth as the salt on the rim of a frozen margarita glass; then, you recognize the familiar bitter sensation that results from worrying about your instructional staffing needs for the coming school year.

It is already June 14, and, despite all of your efforts, you are once again facing the same problem. Your budget provides for ninety-six certified teachers. As of today, you have sixty-eight, possibly sixty-nine (one had knee surgery past week and may or may not return for fall), teachers on staff for the fall. Of these sixty-eight teachers, eleven are either temporarily certified or teaching outside of their area of certification. On top of that, early projections from the district estimate that your student population may increase from 1,080 to 1,200 (the dividends from high test scores). If this increase occurs, you will need to hire an additional eight to ten teachers.

The frustrating thing is that after spending all last summer hiring twenty-three new teachers, you sat down with your staff and developed a plan to avoid the same problem this year. As a result of that meeting, your team planned and implemented the following:

1. Representatives from your school attended five recruiting fairs.
2. You sent letters and district application forms to local colleges of education.
3. Your staff networked through your teachers, parents, colleagues, and friends.

Leadership and Human Resources Development 13

   4. The interview and selection process began early and involved a variety of personnel.
   5. High standards were set for applicants in order to be considered.
   6. Visits by teacher applicants were carefully planned to highlight the strengths of the school—including lunch at a local restaurant.
   7. You offered positions early with guarantees of teaching assignments and classrooms.
   8. A special "new teacher meeting" was held to orient new teachers to the school.
   9. Each new teacher was assigned an experienced mentor.
   10. You allowed each new teacher two "practice" assessment observations before conducting the observations that actually counted.
   11. You increased the "staff development" budget to provide outstanding, exciting, and relevant speakers.

Regardless of this effort, the instructional personnel problem is worse this summer than it was past summer. In response, you assigned one of your APs the task of evaluating past year's efforts and analyzing the reasons for the current crises. You just received the report. A summary of past year's efforts includes a response to each of the eleven separate initiatives attempted last year:

   1. The recruiting fairs were disappointing because there were too many schools represented, only a few top quality applicants, and it was difficult to differentiate your school from the others.
   2. Some applications did result but most of the students coming out of college were hired by the school where they did their student teaching.
   3. Networking seemed to fall by the wayside, especially as the school year progressed.
   4. Early interviewing and hiring worked well for the five positions you knew about and were allowed to search for in December. District transfer provisions froze most positions until May.
   5. The assumption that high standards would attract top people seems to have been a mistake. Few applicants met the high standards set.
   6. This also (see point 4) worked well for a few applicants and over half (five of nine) brought in accepted a position.
   7. Same as point 6.
   8. The meeting was conducted. Although, when we recently asked several teachers about the value of the session, they could not recall the meeting.
   9. A few mentor teachers were supportive of the new teachers; however, as the year progressed, almost no mentoring occurred.

10. The administrative staff got way behind their classroom observations and there was a rush at the end of the year to finish them; thus, many new teachers did not get their practice observations.
11. Feedback on the speakers was very high; however, there was little observable impact on teacher job performance or satisfaction.

The AP's report also summarized and analyzed the numbers for the current crises:

- You started past year with ninety-six full-time certified (a few with temporary) instructional personnel.
- Thirty-eight of these teachers are not returning:
  - Three teachers retired at the end of this year.
  - Four of the twenty-eight new teachers hired last year did not receive a contract renewal.
  - Five of the remaining twenty-four teachers decided they did not really want to be teachers.
  - Thirteen experienced teachers resigned (several were "counseled out" because of poor teaching, two resigned to raise children, two decided to be full-time graduate students, and four moved from the area).
  - Two teachers received administrative appointments in the district.
  - One recently passed away from cancer.
  - Two requested transfer to a different school.
  - Eight were reassigned by the district to a new middle school.
- Six new teachers have been accepted as inner-district transfers.
- Five new teachers have been hired from January 1 to March 31.
- As of January 1, we knew of fifteen openings (ten were locked because other teachers in the district had expressed written interest in those positions under the district transfer policy); as of April 1, there were twenty-one openings; and as of June 14 (today), there were twenty-seven openings!
- From May 1 to June 11, Human Resources (HR) at the Central Office has sent us thirty-two applications that meet their minimal requirements. Fourteen of those meet our stated minimal requirements. Of those fourteen, we have been able to contact eleven, and of those, nine are still interested in visiting our school.
- HR expects to be able to send us an additional fifty to seventy files through the remainder of the summer.

Prompts:

1. What is the problem, if any?
2. What effect does the high teacher attrition rate have on teaching and learning?

> 3. What types of attrition does a school leader have control over?
> 4. What types of attrition does a school leader not have control over?
> 5. What are some of the costs (think in terms of all types of resources available to schools) resulting from teacher attrition?
> 6. Where does leadership fit into all of this?

CHALLENGES AND OPPORTUNITIES OF HRD

The role of the principal is characterized by three consistent and overlapping roles: management, leadership, and administration. Almost everything a principal does in his or her professional practice includes elements of each of the following:

Management—to manage operations, systems, safety, facilities, planning, schedules, and bureaucratic processes.
Administration (to minister to)—to serve, support, meet needs of, provide resources, and provide security.
Leadership—to motivate, inspire, build culture, model, symbolize, teach, learn, and collaboratively develop and communicate a vision.

For example, the frequent role of disciplinarian assigned to APs as a management function is often viewed as separate from instructional leadership; yet the role of a disciplinarian also serves and supports teachers and protects a climate for effective instruction. The quality of work performed by a disciplinarian may either build or decay the culture through the symbolic meaning of every decision made. So it is with HRD, recruiting, hiring, and inducting teachers; coordinating the assessment of teaching and learning; leading professional growth; and dealing with marginal performance all have components of management, administration, and leadership. Leading sustained and effective HRD in a school is a tremendous challenge; however, HRD is also an opportunity to transform an organization. In fact, it is doubtful an organization can perform at high levels without strong leadership in HRD. Nonetheless, the effective development of HR may be the most difficult leadership task facing school administrators because of the following reasons:

- The role of administrator as supporter and evaluator.
- The tension between bureaucratic control and professional autonomy of teachers.
- The complexity of teaching and learning.
- The complexity of school cultures.
- Conflicts between broad reform initiatives and agendas.

- The primary role instructional personnel play in raising student achievement.
- Poor teacher assessment instruments, practices, and training.
- Incompatibility of summative and formative teacher assessment.
- Limited resources (time and money) to provide for a large number of critical HR needs (recruitment, hiring, induction, assessment, and staff development; and dealing with marginal teachers).

The purpose of this chapter is to link HRD and leadership. Clearly, leadership challenges are imminent and daunting. Thus, the focus is on collective leadership and building organizational capacity. This is not the job for one leader to command; rather, it is the job of all professional educators for a school to succeed. This book summarizes a comprehensive framework for school leaders to practice improving organizational performance based on evidence. Professional educators have an ethical obligation to practice the latest advances in research as a physician would with the latest advances in medicine. Therefore, this introductory chapter closes with an overview of the meaning and role of theoretical research in the field of K-12 leadership to ground the relevance and meaning of the content.

EDUCATIONAL THEORY

Sadly, and unfortunately, for educational improvement, there is a divide between individuals who work in schools of education in institutions of higher education and professional practitioners in prekindergarten (PreK)-12 schools. This divide is often articulated as a gulf between the theoretical scholars in the academy and the people who actually perform and live day to day in the "real" world of schools (i.e., theory vs. practice). This divide exists because the organizational cultures in institutions of higher learning and K-12 schools are quite different and, in a real sense, there is a similar but different language in each type of organization. This said, there are some basic misconceptions.

One problem is a simple misunderstanding in regard to the term *theory*. The knowledge base in the field of education includes little true theory in a technical-scientific or social-scientific sense. A theory is a model that describes a relationship (usually cause and effect) between two or more variables consistently (universally) supported by experience (experimentation). A theory is a description, a representation, or a re-presentation of observed natural phenomena and/or social behavior. Educational research rarely produces results consistent with this technical definition. There are two reasons: first, it is almost impossible to conduct pure experimental educational research with true random sampling and random assignments to treatment and control groups, and second, there is almost never universal consistency in educational behavior or contexts.

Regardless of these limitations, educational research is both important and practical, and the value and limitations of educational research need to be understood. Educational research has provided a wealth of knowledge about curriculum, pedagogy, school organizations, social contexts of schools, and leadership. Nevertheless, the field of education remains focused on identifying what works as if once we find the golden egg, schools will suddenly solve existing problems. Such a naïve utopianism does not serve us as educational professionals well in the current milieu of complex social, political, economic, and technical challenges that we face as humans living in the twenty-first century.

Yes, the accumulated body of research in the fields of both leadership and pedagogy is rich, complex, and effective. Regrettably, the gap between the research knowledge base and common professional practice in both pedagogy and leadership remains extensive. Nonetheless, there is a tremendous amount of high quality and beneficial research in education that is not known and/or utilized in practice. The challenge is identifying quality research and implementing the results in practice. A hindrance to this effort is the broad range of the quality of educational research. Some research is poorly conducted, politically and value-laden, and/or poorly written and presented.

In addition, much research is misinterpreted and misused. To sort through the morass of research available, the metaphor of a "map" to think about research is helpful. Research seeks to describe, hopefully a description that is worth something, processes and relationships in educational contexts and practices. Like theories, research represents actual experience or realities, but (and this often gets forgotten) research does not reproduce or become the experience or reality. When you open a map on your phone, you believe the image will represent the actual physical geographical reality you need, and you expect that it is an accurate representation. You do not want a map showing the location of the rain when you need to know the way to Columbus nor do you need a map with the roads mislabeled and/or situated in the wrong place. Thus, it makes no more sense to talk about differences between theory and practice than it does to talk about the difference between a map on a smartphone of the state of Ohio and the physical state of Ohio. On the other hand, it makes considerable sense to talk about the purpose and the quality of the map.

If you read an educational research study, or any writings on education, and it does not fit with your experience and reality of practice, the research is either of poor quality or being misapplied in some manner. In conclusion, you should engage the content and discussions of this text with a critical eye, not with the intention of proving those in the "ivory tower" are too full of theory to find a classroom but to help us, and yourself, to produce better and more useful maps of the "real" world of teaching, learning, and leading in schools.

CONCLUSION

This chapters presents key constructs of organizational leadership from a lens of HRD practice. The key point is the role of leadership in mediating the relationship between the governance, policies, and bureaucratic systems of K-12 public education and the professional practitioners actually performing the work, primarily teachers. While there are different ways to view this work, this chapter suggests there is little a K-12 school leader does that is not impacted by effective HRD at the building level. The chapter begins with an explanation of this role and the difficulty of balancing the needs of the public system and the profession of teaching to achieve a shared purpose.

The foundational construct for success is a strong positive organizational culture. A strong culture has a large impact on organizational goals and a positive culture improves organizational performance. A short history of the role of culture in organizational theory emphasizes the long-term importance of culture in the field of educational leadership. The key idea is best summarized as an understanding that all systemic improvement efforts, no matter how innovative or supported by research they may be, depend on the knowledge, skill, and motivation of the people implementing them.

The second essential characteristic of this chapter argues the primary tool a school leader has available to improve teaching and learning is effective HRD. The key is linking the separate HRD functions in to a single focus on improving teacher quality. Beginning with effective recruiting, a school will have a better pool of applicants to select teachers from. Good hiring decisions followed with effective new teacher induction will increase teacher retention and effectively develop new teachers. Finally, focused assessment of teaching and learning supporting targeted teacher developed and teacher led professional growth will facilitate all teachers' achieving their full potential.

The chapter concludes with an overview of theory in the field of educational leadership. The content in this book is supported by research-based assumptions regarding organizational behavior, and the relationship between leadership and teaching on student learning. The key here is a need for practitioners to understand both the value and limitations of research in supporting the real work of educating children performed by school-based educational professionals every day. Chapter Two presents *cost effective and efficient HRD* and presents economic theory as a key research-based theoretical foundation of this book.

Chapter 2

Economic Theory and Developing Human Resources

INTRODUCTION

Human resource development is examined as an economic process for an important reason—education is an intensely human economic enterprise. From the perspective of HRD, teachers are the primary resource in providing the service of teaching to produce learning to the children in our communities. This chapter approaches the work of professional educational practitioners as a resource in the delivery (production) of teaching and learning services. This is not some crass attempt to suggest that the work of teachers is akin to a machine; rather, it is a recognition and appreciation of the value of the work of teachers.

A theoretical lens based on economics provides a framework for analyzing and describing administrative and leadership practice to acquire the knowledge and ability to gain the most value from the professional work of teachers through organizational development. Individuals who practice in the public education profession receive taxpayers' money to provide educational services to communities. The public money for education includes not only professional salaries but also all the money spent by school districts to educate children.

While there are many ways to view the roles in the profession (principal, teacher, and support service provider), it is nonetheless the responsibility of all educators to use public resources wisely to obtain the most educational value per dollar of taxpayer funds. The role of HRD is central to an organization's ability to maximize the *efficient* use of *HR*.

There is a key economic concept in the previous sentence. In economics, *efficiency* means operating without waste in a manner producing the highest possible level of output (production) with a given level of input (resources). Efficiency may be used to describe the operation of a machine, an individual worker, a group of workers, or an organization. In economic terms, organizations (including schools) exist to *produce goods* and *services*.

A *good* is a tangible object one can touch and a *service* is an intangible action with economic (monetary) value that someone, or in case of an organization, does for another individual or organization. As an example, retail supercenters sell goods and hospitals provide health services. Education is a service; however, in economic terms, both goods and services are considered production or product. Economists measure *gross domestic product* as the total value of goods and services produced by a nation in a single year. Included in this calculation are expenditures for education. Translating this back to the economics of education, *efficiency in a school* refers to the production of the most student-learning, given the resources available to the school organization.

This chapter presents several economic principles related to efficiency and HRD. The first is a theoretical examination of the value of teaching through the teacher labor market. The key point is that efficient teachers are able to improve the achievement of children. Effective teachers are a precious asset with a high market value and often have a wide range of professional options. While the work all teachers do with children is valuable, the skills required for teaching different subjects and different levels have different values in the broader labor market.

Thus, it is helpful to examine what conditions in the labor market influence teachers' decisions to remain or leave different types of educational contexts. As an economic comparison, imagine the sale of a used car. Individuals are economically motivated to get the most *value* (money) out of selling a vehicle and, thus, have an incentive to find a buyer willing to pay the highest price. In economic terms, it is no different for a teacher selling his or her professional services to a school; the individual has an economic incentive to get the most value out of his or her services and will seek a buyer (school system, private school, or other options available outside of education) that will offer the highest value (value may be monetary, working conditions, opportunities to make a difference, or other factors depending on each individual) for his or her professional services. The relevant question for educational leaders is: What, along with money, do teachers value to the extent it influences a decision on where, or if, to teach? According to Guarino, Santibañez, and Daley (2006), working conditions is a key variable that influences teachers' decisions on where to seek or accept employment. It is worth noting that working conditions include school culture and other factors directly related to the quality and type of leadership.

The next topic is an overview of costs associated with providing educational services. An estimated 80 percent (Cavanagh, 2017) of all public education expenditures in the United States are used for teachers' salaries and benefits, hiring teachers, assessing teachers, and developing teachers. In addition, there is also a cost of marginal teaching and replacing marginal teachers. When kids do not progress appropriately, it costs money for remediation and necessary supplemental services. Holding a child back from advancing to the next grade requires an extra year of schooling, thirteen years instead of twelve, and this cost alone is approximately $11,000 per student retained each year.

Further, replacing a marginal teacher requires remediation efforts, extensive documentation, and lengthy due-process proceedings—all with considerable expense. The costs of the various elements of HRD are explained to develop an understanding of the use of *opportunity costs* as tool to make resource allocation decisions. Most school organizations tend to focus on the output side of the efficiency equation. In other words, there is a focus on improving test scores. Although school districts and school-based administrators are generally cognizant of budgetary limitations, there is, nonetheless, a tendency in many educational organizations to misunderstand economic issues of limited resources and the relationship between inputs, costs, and processes. Following the analysis of costs, the economic benefits associated with HRD are explained, including the value of effective teachers and effective recruitment, hiring, induction, assessment, and development of instructional personnel. The key construct here is the economic value of teaching services. An understanding of the real market value of teaching services has multiple benefits. Ultimately, the worth of educators is determined by the value society places on the education of its children and the level of influence educators have on the learning of each individual child.

While the resource needs of schools are complex and multifaceted, an understanding of the value of teaching supports an increase in the level of resources dedicated to teacher compensation and to the professional needs of teachers. In other words, from an economic perspective, an argument is presented which posits that funds committed to the compensation, development, and support of teachers are a more efficient use of resources than money spent on whole school reform packages, online curriculum packages, expensive benchmark assessments, and high-priced consultants and professional development providers.

In addition, choosing to focus resources on teachers provides a positive impact on the local economy and produces political goodwill by investing educational dollars within a community. In addition, methods to understand and anticipate the benefits associated with different HRD functions are presented. Finally, this chapter combines an understanding of costs and benefits to support efficient decisions regarding the allocation of scarce resources for HRD functions. How much time and money should be committed to recruiting teachers, hiring teachers, inducting teachers, assessing teachers, and developing teachers? The chapter presents principles of *cost-benefit analysis* as a tool for strategic human resources planning (SHRP) in all areas of HRD. For example, a principal must understand the real costs of an effective induction program in order to justify the time and effort required to obtain the desired retention and growth of new teachers.

TEACHER LABOR MARKETS

Managing for organizational efficiency in a school requires knowledge and understanding of teacher labor markets (getting the most/best teaching for each dollar spent on instructional services). There are several *factors of production*, including land, capital, natural resources, and labor. Capital includes money and tools of production, including buildings, machines, supplies, and technology. In an organization, labor is considered a resource. The key point is humans are economic service providers to organizations.

Thus, teaching services have a *market value* subject to the same economic laws of *supply and demand* as any other good or service in the economic marketplace. In the economic labor market for professional teaching services, *supply* is the number of "qualified" individuals willing to provide teaching services at a given price (salary level or other considerations of value). *Demand* is the number of teachers that schools (districts and/or all schools in a given market—likely a geographical area) will hire at a given price. Thus, in the labor market for teaching services, teachers are the sellers of teaching services and schools are the buyers of the teaching services. Teachers provide (sell) pedagogical and other valuable skills in professional education and non-education labor markets, and professionals in other areas market their skills in the professional education labor market.

The teacher labor market is not a pure free market (open market) because teachers' salaries are largely influenced by a combination of government (school board) control and conditions in the overall labor market. Nonetheless, teachers and school systems have, and make, choices that create conditions of market supply and demand. For example, if a school system offered to pay teachers $100,000 per year, it is likely many individuals with teaching skills and qualifications would apply (not to mention the incentive this would provide individuals to acquire the necessary skills and qualifications), and the result would likely be a *surplus* of teachers in the labor market. On the other hand, if a school system offered to pay teachers $10,000 per year, it is likely that only a few individuals would apply, and there would be a *shortage* of teachers.

Simply, in a market, a shortage of a good or service (including teaching) indicates a price below market value with the shortage pushing prices higher, and a surplus of a good or service indicates a price above market value with the surplus pushing prices lower. The supply and demand of teachers is also influenced by price (salaries) in other labor markets. For example, a teacher with high skill levels in math and technology may be able to sell his or her services in the private sector for a much higher salary or a large number of layoffs in the subprime mortgage industry might result in an increase in the number of individuals willing to teach high school economics at current salary. In addition, there are actually many teacher labor markets characterized by wide variations in professional skill sets.

Different markets vary in the following types of professional skills required: grade level, geographical region, and school type. Because of this, *opportunity costs* for individuals deciding to enter and remain in the profession of teaching vary significantly. According to Cassandra Guarino from the RAND Corporation, the determining factor in teacher supply is *"individuals will become or remain teachers if teaching represents the most attractive activity to pursue among all activities available to them"* (Guarino, Santibañez, & Daley, 2006, p. 175). Given this, it is not surprising that Guarino, et al. (2006) found much evidence that teachers in the field of mathematics and science, and teachers with higher measured academic ability were more likely to leave the profession. A strong factor making teaching attractive for many individuals is the desire to work with children and make a positive difference in society. Teachers as a whole are willing to take less pay for the satisfaction of doing something that benefits children and society.

In addition to the value of a teacher's skills in alternative labor markets, Guarino, et al. (2006) found that working conditions have a large impact on teacher supply. Schools with higher proportions of minority, low-income, and low-performing students tend to have higher teacher attrition rates, and urban schools have higher attrition rates than suburban and rural districts (Guarino, et al., 2006, p. 200). Further, internal variables of school culture and climate also influence teachers' decisions to remain in the classroom. Simply, the services of qualified teachers in some schools cost more than others. Because of working conditions, the same teacher costs more in inner-city schools or schools with hostile or unsupportive cultures. The findings of Guarino, Santibañez, and Daley (2006) were supported by the research conducted by Borman and Dowling (2008) and teacher retention and attrition. Findings of this meta-analysis concluded:

- "First, the attrition from the profession of teaching is not necessarily 'healthy' attrition." (p. 396)
- "Second, attrition appears to be influenced by a number of personal and professional factors that are prone to change across the life span and career path." (p. 396)

- "Third, the characteristics of teachers' work conditions are more salient for predicting attrition than previously noted in the literature." (p. 398)
- "Fourth, there are various conditions, such as higher salaries, teacher collaboration and networking, and administrative support, that are related to retention and that are quite amenable to change." (p. 398)

Case Reflection 2 exemplifies the meaning of this research in practice. The example is consistent with "unhealthy attrition," "personal and professional factors," working conditions relevant to the cultural characteristics of a school, and factors "related to retention that are quite amenable to change".

Case Reflection 2

"Maggie Sells Her Speech Services to a New Buyer"

Maggie is a Speech and Language Pathologist (SLP) doing contract work in a large urban school district. The district has a severe shortage of SLPs and must contract supplemental SLP services through a private agency at a cost to the district of roughly $70 per hour (approximately two-third of this amount is for Maggie's pay, the additional cost includes the agency fee, benefits, and other costs). Maggie is considered extremely effective by colleagues and her supervisor describes her "as the best SLP I have ever observed working with children." In the fall of a new school year, Maggie was once again assigned to a high-needs elementary school she had worked in during the previous year and a half. She was the only SLP at the school and had an overload of students. Nonetheless, the school was required by law to provide speech and language services to each child on her caseload. As a member of the professional staff, Maggie agreed to assist with morning bus duty one day a week for one hour before school and afternoon bus duty every day for thirty minutes. She was glad to be part of the professional team at the school. The practice of SLP's is highly specialized and includes extensive testing, assessment, individual and small group sessions with students, extensive paperwork, and record-keeping. It is standard practice in most schools and districts for SLPs to develop their own schedules in consultation with classroom teachers. In previous years at the beginning of the school year, Maggie met with teachers and, following considerable effort and negotiation, was able to work out a schedule that allowed her to provide SLP services to all of the students on her caseload without removing them from class during critical times of numeracy and literacy instruction.

Two weeks into the school year, an AP asked Maggie to come to her office. The AP explained to Maggie that she was needed for lunch duty three days per week. Maggie was willing to do the lunch duty; however, after going through her schedule, she could not find a way to change her schedule that would enable her to provide all of the services required by law without removing children from class during critical instructional time. Maggie reported to the AP that she could not rearrange her schedule to do the lunch duty. The following day, Maggie was told by the AP that she was a "contract worker" and that she needed to "be a team player and work it out" if she wanted to continue working in the school. Later that day, Maggie was given a revised schedule the AP had created for her. Maggie's first reaction was to express concern that the new schedule did not fit with the schedules of the classroom teachers. At this point, Maggie spent three-and-a-half hours in the AP's office while the AP contacted each individual teacher and told the teachers to adjust daily schedules so Maggie could pull students out of class for SLP services during noncritical instructional times. The following day, many teachers expressed negative feelings because they had to redo their schedules so a small percentage of students could receive speech and language services. Maggie felt she was not being treated as a professional and she was being unfairly treated by the administration—a situation she was unwilling to tolerate. That night, Maggie contacted her supervisor and her agency to discuss the situation. Maggie felt a strong professional commitment to complete her assignment but she was concerned with her ability to effectively provide services in her current situation. The agency she worked for offered to place another SLP into the school and place her in a school in another district in the same city. Although Maggie was devastated and distraught at abandoning the children she served, some that she had worked with for over a year, she reported to her new school the next day.

Questions:

1. From the administrators' point of view, what HR management processes were evident in this case?
2. The school/district Maggie worked in was willing to pay $70/hour for a highly skilled professional practitioner to watch children in a lunchroom. Is this an efficient use of resources? What other alternatives, if any, are available to school-based administrators?
3. What specific economic constructs related to HR are relevant in the situation described in the case?
4. How might effective planning prevent situations from occurring similar to the one described in the case?

The construct of HRD is an overall strategy designed to ensure that an organization meets its essential goals. More than any other aspect, HRD is an approach that defines the relationship between the organization and the individuals in the organization. In a nutshell, the principles of HRD are deeply connected to leadership. How might HRD influence an organization's approach to how they deal with professional service providers or how might a focus on HRD influence leadership? In regard to Maggie's situation in the case, her decision to leave the school may be described in economic terms. In this case, the alternatives available to Maggie became more attractive than her current situation.

As an SLP in a labor market with a shortage of SLPs and high demand in the private sector for noneducational SLP services, Maggie had a wide range of alternative choices available. She had a choice of moving to another school or offering her services in the high-paying private sector. This is a true case and, in her city, an experienced SLP working in a rehabilitation hospital would earn a six-figure income. Yet the deciding factor for Maggie was not salary; rather, it was working conditions stemming from mismanaged HRD. It does not appear that the leadership in Maggie's school did a good job of planning for the efficient use of the available Time.

This had a direct impact on working conditions for Maggie, and her departure will likely further degrade the efficiency of the school organization. Perhaps the school leaders failed to provide Maggie the value she needed, not in terms of salary, but rather in terms of working conditions necessary to her in exchange for her services. The bottom line is that individual members of a school's professional staff have, and do in fact make, choices. Teachers with knowledge and skills of high value in the private sector tend to have more attractive alternatives in terms of both salary and working conditions. Simply, in schools where teachers do not want to work because of poor working conditions, teachers with skills enabling them to find attractive alternatives often avail themselves of these alternatives. These schools risk ending up with a teaching force of professionals with, for various reasons, no other options in comparable labor markets. Thus, schools may end up with teachers who have no other equivalent job opportunities.

In conclusion, for a school leader striving to improve the quality of the professionals working in the school through hiring and retaining quality faculty members, many things matter relative to the local teacher labor market:

- the salary and benefit package;
- the community both in the neighborhood of the school and the surrounding areas;
- the professional culture in the school;
- opportunities for professional growth and advancement;

- working conditions, including security, student behavioral norms, teaching loads, classroom assignments, availability of instructional resources, and duty assignments;
- the physical conditions of the buildings and grounds;
- community support and engagement;
- the opportunity to make a difference;
- the type and behavior of building-level leadership; and
- mentoring and collegial support.

COSTS

Opportunity cost is an economic concept used to account for choices not selected. Opportunity cost represents the available options not selected when decisions on resources utilization (money is spent, time is used, buildings are utilized) are made. For example, if an individual was to win $100,000 in the lottery and decides to go out and buy a new BMW, the opportunity cost of the choice is all of the other possible things he or she could have done with the money. He or she would have lost the opportunity to use the money to send a child to college (of course, he or she still might be able to pay to send a child to college but not with the lottery money).

In economics, the lost opportunities are considered to be a real cost. The real cost of lost opportunities is evident when you think about the operation of schools. Every dollar spent on textbooks is dollar not available to spend on technology. Every dollar spent on substitute teachers is a dollar not spent on professional development. Every hour a teacher spends on duty or in a faculty meeting is an hour not spent on providing instruction. In Maggie's case, her school (district) was spending $70 per hour for her to supervise children before and after school three-and-a-half hours per week ($245/week), and the school wanted to increase her duty time to six-and-a-half hours per week at a direct cost of $455/week or $16,380 per year! More importantly, however, the six-and-a-half hours that Maggie would have been spending on duty would have been six-and-a-half hours per week or 234 hours per year that Maggie would not have been providing SLP services to kids. In schools, *any activity that takes teachers away from providing instruction has an extremely high opportunity cost.*

A good example of opportunity cost in making HRD decisions is mentoring. Mentoring is extremely valuable for beginning teachers and has been shown to greatly increase new teacher performance and retention (Ingersoll & Strong, 2011; Smith & Ingersoll, 2004). However, mentoring is also extremely expensive, especially in terms of time; thus, there is a high opportunity cost consisting of other possible uses of the time. Successful mentoring programs require extensive mentor training, extended duration (two years is optimal), release time for classroom observation and assessment (mentor observing the mentee, and the mentee observing the mentor), and release time for consultation and shared planning. The question is: Is the cost worth it comparted to other uses of limited professional time? SHRP provides a process to assess real "costs" of HRD and other operational functions and procedures, and to make decisions based on anticipated benefits. This is called *cost-benefit analysis* and it is an essential tool for effective HR planning.

COST-BENEFIT ANALYSIS AND SHRP

Cost-benefit analysis is a decision-making tool common in effective SHRP. It allows the comparison of various alternatives and a mechanism for determining opportunity costs for key decisions—This is a simple litmus test used to make decisions that provide the most benefit per unit of cost (usually dollars or time). The first part of the process is to estimate cost. Weak and ineffective HR management in schools is almost always the result of insufficient resources (time and money) and rarely a result of "how to" knowledge. In other words, poor teacher recruiting and hiring, poor new teacher induction, poor teaching evaluation, poor professional development, and failure to adequately deal with ineffective instruction are primarily a result of limited time and money. Most schools could do a much better job recruiting teachers if they had a full-time recruiter with an unlimited budget. The same goes for hiring. Imagine if you had the time and money to bring the top three applicants for a teaching position to your school, you could put them up at the finest local hotel; take them out for meals at fine restaurants; provide them opportunities to meet the students, faculty, and parents; and have them teach a lesson or two to in the classroom (this is common practice in higher education and the private sector). Chances are higher that you would make better hiring decisions and top applicants would be more likely to select your school among other choices. HR processes are expensive, especially in terms of time.

The key point is that professional time is a cost (time is money). Nationally, the average hourly cost to school systems for professional services is $40 per hour for base salaries and an additional $12 per hour for benefits. This amount is based on an average teacher salary in the United States in 2018 of approximately $60,000 (McCarthy, 2019) divided by 180 days, divided by 8 hours per day, equaling $41.67. Benefits add approximately 30 percent, raising the amount by $12 for a total of $52 per hour. Thus, if a school with fifty teachers has a one-hour faculty meeting, the cost of that faculty meeting, in real taxpayer dollars spent, is $2,600. School-based administrators often do not view professional time as a direct cost and therefore utilize this time in highly inefficient ways. At the district level, teacher salaries tend to be a *variable cost* (a cost of production that varies depending on the level of production—if you have more students, you will need more teachers and salary costs will increase). At the school level, however, professional time is more of a *fixed cost* (a cost of production that remains constant regardless of production levels—a building must be paid for whether it has 500 students in or a 1,000), during a given school year. Thus, from the school administrator's point of view, it is budgetary money already spent—calling a faculty meeting does not take any additional money out of the principal's budget.

BENEFITS OF EFFECTIVE HRD

The economic benefits of effective HRD are many and include reduced costs, increased output, efficiency, and organizational coherency. Regardless, this discussion is not about producing widgets in a factory or providing entertainment at a rock concert. Rather, a school administrator who reduces costs is saving the hard-earned tax dollars of the citizens of his or her district. Increasing output means better preparing the children of a community for life achievement. Efficiency involves balancing what will always be limited resources with maximum learning. It is not about grouping kids and standardizing curricula and assessments; rather, the task is to meet the individual learning needs of each child while avoiding wasteful expenditures of time and resources. Coherency is, as Fullan and Quinn (2016) explain, aligning the right drivers for educational change. In schools, it is professional educators who make coherency happen. There is nothing more important to the success of a school in accomplishing its purpose than the work of professional educators. An economic lens is a tool to support coherency, but, to be an effective tool, HRD must be utilized in a manner that supports a healthy, professional, collaborative, and learning organizational culture. Edwards Deming (1986), the father of data-based decision-making, also emphasized the essential humanity of economic thinking and included admonitions in his "14 Points" including calls to "cease dependence on inspection to achieve quality," "institute leadership," "eliminate quotas," "remove barriers that rob people of pride of workmanship," "eliminate slogans and exhortations," "institute education and self-improvement," and "put everybody to work to accomplish the transformation." Thus, from a perspective of the economic benefits of HRD, economic theory is a guide to obtain the shared purpose of the people in the organization.

Thus, the core benefits of effective HRD in a school are the creation of an organization and place that people (students, teachers, staff, administrators, parents, and community members) want to be a part of and spend precious moments of one's life. This is easy to say or write, but what is the value of this type of school: What is it worth? There are techniques for estimating through measurement the productive value of various levels of education, but the meaning and value of an education transcends monetary calculation. What is the value of enjoying one's work or one's educational experience? What is the value of a great school to a community? Effective HRD is akin to a form of maintenance. Diligent attention to the details and initial investment of time and resources will keep a vehicle operating smoothly and maintain its value. Likewise, in HRD, diligent attention to recruiting, hiring, inducting, assessing, and developing teachers will keep the school running smoothly and its productive output (value) high. An initial investment and intensive focus on HRD will result in a lower need and less cost for HRD functions in the future. On the other hand, like a blown engine, a dysfunctional ineffective school organization void of HRD is an expensive repair.

Planning, the focus of the next chapter, is the key to maximizing the benefits of HRD. A well-thought-out recruiting plan implemented with fidelity will target potential teachers and provide the information they need and an easy process for communicating interest, asking questions, and submitting an application. If implemented correctly, this will result in a high number of qualified applicants from a reasonable recruiting expenditure. A strong pool of applicants will have a beneficial impact on the selection process. A selection and hiring process supported by a range of valid quantitative and trustworthy qualitative data organized for easy access and assessment will not only be cost effective, but it will also support the selection of the highest qualified applicant. This type of process will also present a positive image of the school encouraging the individual selected to take the job. Further, engaging stakeholders in collaborative processes to recruit and select teachers will support the development of a positive culture. New hires will be viewed as individuals that "we" want to be a part of what "we" are doing. Finally, the experiences of an effective hiring process will transition nicely into effective induction of onboarding teachers.

Chapter 6 focuses on best practices for new teacher induction but, from a benefit lens, these practices focus on assessing and addressing the needs of new teachers to promote improving performance and facilitating retention. Certainly, best practices in new teacher induction are expensive but the potential benefits are transformative. First, effective new teacher induction is a community effort with all stakeholders committed to and collaborating for the success of new teachers. The most import aspect is for the community to model the positive cultural norms expected of professional behavior, communication, and interaction. As stated earlier, the value of culture is difficult to measure but, to the extent that culture influences productivity, it is extremely high. In addition, losing a teacher and then recruiting, selecting, hiring, and inducting a new teacher is expensive.

A study (Barnes, Crowe, & Schaefer, 2007) conducted over a decade ago on the cost of replacing a teacher in five large districts reported a low-cost estimate of $4,365 per teacher and a higher cost estimate of $9,501 per teacher. In today's dollars based on average teacher salary, this estimate becomes a low of $5,552 and a high of $12,088 to replace each teacher. Ingersoll, Merrill, and Stuckey (2014) report multiple disturbing trends related to the cost of replacing teachers. In 2008–2009, 13 percent of the 3.4 million teachers in America changed schools (227,016) or left the profession (230,122). In addition, schools serving students in high-poverty lose approximately 20 percent of their teaching force each year. In addition, Ingersoll, Merrill, and Stuckey (2014) reported between 1993 and 2003 that an average of 41.3 percent of all teachers nationwide left each school.

This results in an annual cost of between $1 billion (low estimate) and $2.2 billion (high estimate) per year in 2009 US dollars. In Mississippi, the state with the highest poverty rate in the nation, an estimated 3,500 left the profession out of a teaching force of just under 35,000 (10 percent). This cost the state a low estimate of $15,350,000 and a high estimate of $33,500,000 (Ingersoll, Merrill, & Stuckey 2014). Given these data, a high-poverty school hiring twenty new teachers in a school year will lose four of the new teachers. On the other hand, if a high-poverty school with an effective hiring and induction program retained three of the teachers who would otherwise have left, the school will save between $16,500 and $36,000 that year alone. If through effective HRD, the same school was able to cut the five-year attrition rate in half, from losing over sixty teachers to thirty teachers (Ingersoll, Merrill, and Stuckey [2014] report high-poverty schools on average may lose 60 percent of teachers in five years), the school will save between $330,000 and $720,000 to utilize on other needs instead of replacing teachers. While important, these benefits of effective hiring and recruiting focus on cost savings; however, the primary benefit from an economic perspective is improved teaching performance and increased learning (production).

While improvement in teaching is difficult to measure because once a teacher improves due to development efforts, it is difficult to know how the teacher would have performed with there was no development. Improvement is, nonetheless, a real and tangible economic benefit of effective hiring, induction, and other HRD processes. One key benefit from improved teaching resulting from induction, assessment, and development is a reduction of the number of students retained each year. An easy way to conceptualize this is to use the average cost per student per year in a school or district. If the average cost is $11,000 per year and child is required to repeat third grade, then the price is an additional $11,000 to repay an expenditure (the child's third grade year) already incurred.

Thus, if a teacher is able to produce results that prevent students from repeating grades, each struggling student the teacher advances is saving the school and district a large amount of money. In the end, there are several ways to conceptualize and measure the output benefits of improved learning but, in the end, the benefits accrue from changes in behavior of teachers in the classroom that result in increased learning. The processes covered in this book are designed to improve teaching; thus, this chapter closes with research (Hanushek, 2011) estimating the benefit of improved teaching.

CONCLUSION

If a school is able to replace a departing marginal teacher with an effective teacher in terms of student learning produced, the benefits are significant. Hanushek (2011) explains these benefits well at the micro (school or classroom) and macro (national) levels:

> A teacher one standard deviation above the mean effectiveness annually generates marginal gains of over $400,000 in present value of student future earnings with a class size of 20 and proportionately higher with larger class sizes. Alternatively, replacing the bottom 5–8 percent of teachers with average teachers could move the U.S. near the top of international math and science rankings with a present value of $100 trillion.

This chapter began with evidence that instructional costs relating to teacher performance account for around 80 percent (Cavanagh, 2017) of a school's budget. Most of these costs cover the salaries and benefits paid to teachers. Another large portion covers the HRD functions discussed here, including recruiting, hiring, inducting, assessing, and developing teachers.

As stated, the primary purpose in these introductory chapters is to center HRD processes in not only administrative practice but also teacher leadership and the culture of the school. The argument presented in this chapter assumes the costs of effective HRD are high, especially in terms of time; thus, HRD demands a high level of individual and organizational commitment. Regardless, with an HRD focus on improving teaching and learning, the costs become consistent with the organizational mission and the purpose of professionals working in schools. In the end, the benefits far outweigh the costs as the results may best be understood as progress toward the realization of the school's vision and mission.

Chapter 3

Strategic Planning for Developing Human Resources

INTRODUCTION

Strategic Human Resources Planning is a comprehensive planning process, including all areas of organizational and operational planning. The framework for the process is an intentional focus on organizational performance (output) and human behavior (processes and resources). The term *strategic* identifies the process as a holistic, comprehensive, and all-inclusive effort to develop a plan for the achievement of the organization's mission. It is the highest level of planning in an organization. In other words, you might have many subcategories or plans that fit under the strategic plan but there is no higher plan at the building level than the SHRP.

An HR focus allows an organization to achieve its mission by preparing for the efficient utilization of professional staff. The planning process must be consistent with the organization's mission as articulated in the *mission statement*. The mission statement is a concise description of the reason the school exists as an institution (McQueen & Burnham, 2015). In other words, a mission statement articulates the primary purpose of the organization. It is helpful to keep three principles in mind when developing a vision statement: schools serve children, schools belong to the community, and schools are centers of teaching and learning. When mission statements are imposed on a professional staff from administrators, they have little cultural relevance and often convey negative symbolic meaning (members may view the statements as cliché, trite, trivial, and/or silly).

This is also true when previous, or old, mission statements are simply passed on. Meaningful mission statements are developed through a team effort involving representatives from stakeholders within the school and in the community. A strategic plan with an HR focus requires *strategic objectives*.

Strategic objectives should articulate the immediate and long-term HRD of the school that are consistent with the mission statement. In other words, in order to achieve the purpose of the organization, what relationship is required between the organization and the people who are part of it? The determination of strategic objectives for HRD is accomplished by considering several structural and process questions.

Structural Questions:

- What type of professional practitioner do we need to accomplish the objectives?
- How many instructional and staff positions will we need and in what areas?
- What resources do we have available to commit to HR?
- When will resources be available?
- How will we maximize the efficient use of available resources?
- Who will be involved in HR processes and decision-making and why?

Process Questions:

- How will we identify and hire the best teachers/personnel?
- How might we successfully bring new people into the organization?
- How might we assess priority needs in order to improve teaching and learning?
- How might we provide the most effective professional development for all instructional and noninstructional personnel?
- How will we deal with personnel issues, especially marginal instruction?

While the structural questions are more predetermined and theoretical, the answers to the process questions directly translate into the day-to-day operation of the school.

There are fairly standard procedures for answering the process questions. The first step is to collectively engage in a *gap analysis*. A gap analysis is a tool for discovering where the organization stands at the current time and comparing the current status to where it needs to be (the strategic objectives). The gap analysis requires the collection or use of internal school data (see examples of the use of gap analyses data in chapter 9, tables 9.1 to 9.3). Using the example of a new teacher induction program, data are collected to assess current new teacher induction practices. It is important that the data also be collected on the effectiveness of the current practices. In collecting these data, there may be some quantitative measures available; however, the most useful understanding of current practices will come from informal or formal (planned) *observations and conversations*.

There needs to be meaningful conversations with new teachers about their induction and intentional observation of induction activities. The next step in the SHRP process is to develop and implement strategies for eliminating the identified gaps. It is essential that the strategies be developed collaboratively and be supported by data, both from within and from outside the school. Thus, research on effective new teacher induction should be utilized and combined with the type of new teacher induction needed and desired in the school. The key to successful implementation of a revised new teacher induction program is buy-in and ownership by the professional staff and other stakeholders.

The final step in the planning process is an *assessment plan* to specify how the new teacher induction program will be monitored and assessed. Key elements of the assessment plan must identify what data will be collected, when and how it will be collected and maintained, and how the data will be used to improve the program and inform future decision-making. With this overview of planning for strategic planning, the next section provides detailed guidelines for the actual process.

CONDUCTING STRATEGIC PLANNING

Successful strategic planning, including SHRP, is a collaborative process involving stakeholders representing teachers, community members, parents, staff, and even students. It is important that all individuals affected by the plan have a voice in the development of the plan. When stakeholders are involved in the plan, there is ownership and commitment to the subsequent implementation of the ideals. When strategic decisions are made in secret by a few administrators, there is little initial buy-in resulting in difficulties in implementation of the plan. Following is a simple step-by-step team approach to strategic planning in public education developed by Doug McQueen and Tom Burnham (2015; Burnham, 2019). Doug McQueen and Tom Burnham both have extensive experience in school leadership and strategic planning:

> **Doug McQueen** began his career as a teacher, later serving as a principal in the Biloxi Public Schools and assistant superintendent in the Harrison County Schools. As an educator, he was an early adopter of staff development, later named professional development. This interest resulted in his accepting a position with Mississippi Power Company as a business trainer. He was later hired by Scientific Methods to conduct national and international training on the leadership model, Managerial Grid. Prior to joining the University of Mississippi, Doug served as Director of Training for Central and Southwest Public Utility and American Electric Power. In these roles he authored numerous training materials and with co-author Tory Herring authored and published "The Brutus

Dilemma, and Betrayal in the Workplace." Throughout his career, he continued to work with local school districts across the country on strategic planning and leadership development. (Burnham, 2019)

Tom Burnham is a career leader in education serving as high school principal, district superintendent in Mississippi and North Carolina, two-time Mississippi Superintendent of Education, Dean of the School of Education at the University of Mississippi, and Director of the Mississippi Principal Corps.

Schools or districts using the *Guidelines for Strategic Planning* developed by McQueen and Burnham (2015) may either adapt the steps to focus on SHRP for a district or include HRD processes into a comprehensive strategic plan at the building level. Ideally, the district will complete this process first to allow building-level principals a framework and model to ensure the school-level plan is consistent with the district processes and approved strategic plan.

GUIDELINES TO STRATEGIC PLANNING
DOUG MCQUEEN AND TOM BURNHAM (2015)

Step One: A strategic plan at either the district or school level should involve a minimum of two teams. For school level, one team includes school administrators and other members of the leadership team (district administrators and school board members at the district level). A second team should include stakeholders in the school, or district, and community. Stakeholders may be best utilized in multiple teams: principal and school administrators, faculty, parents, and community members. An ideal session will include around twenty, but not exceeding thirty, participants in two to four teams (four to six teams at the district level). In separate conversations, each team is asked to brainstorm a list to describe what "super success" for the school or district looks like. Following this, the teams are brought together to share ideas and develop a fully agreed-upon final list. The collective teams then use this list to generate a vision statement. Existing mission statements should then be revised, or a new mission statement created. According to McQueen and Burnham (2015), "The vision statement describes where the school or district wants to be. The mission statement describes the purpose of the organization, why it exists." If one does not exist, a list of five to eight values for the school or district needs to be articulated. McQueen and Burnham provide several examples:

- *We believe that all students and staff should have a safe and healthy environment.*

- *We believe that all children can learn.*
- *We believe that all students should receive quality instruction in every class.*

Once all of the teams agree on what "super success" looks like (a vision statement, a mission statement, and list of core values) the next step involves describing the school or district as it is today.

Step Two: Teams again work independently to brainstorm a list of statements to describe the school or district as it is today. As in step one, once each team has developed a list of descriptors, the teams then come together as a single group and reach common agreement on the current status of the school or district by comparing the list of what "super success" looks like and the list of current attributes that typically result in gaps between where the school or districts wants to be and where it actually is.

Step Three: Teams again work together to discuss barriers to "super success" and then share them with the large group. The group then agrees on a list of the five most important barriers standing between where the school, or district, is and where the group members want it to be. The final step is the creation of statement of goals to minimize or remove the five barriers to success. The group should limit the number of goals to no more than five in order to keep the strategic plan manageable. *The products at the conclusion of step three constitute the core components of the strategic plan: Vision, Mission, Values, and Goals.*

Step Four: Develop a set of objectives. This may be done in a new set of teams focusing on one to three objectives for each goal. The teams are directed to think about the objectives as the steps necessary to accomplish the goal. Each step needs to be articulated in a manner that success can be measured. Once a set of measurable objectives is agreed upon, *a first draft of the strategic plan is completed.* At this point, it is wise to share the draft with other stakeholders and seek input on additions or changes. This is also a time when the draft should be submitted to the central office or school board for approval.

Step Five: With approval of the draft strategic plan, a separate session using school (for school-level planning) or district (for district-level planning) personnel develops one to five action items necessary to accomplish each objective. The action items should be described with measureable outcomes. Personnel are then assigned responsibilities to implement and monitor the action items. For school-level planning, central office personnel should not be included in this step to avoid role confusion between school-based decisions and central office policy, monitoring, and support. District planning should likewise avoid school board involvement during this stage to avoid blurring the distinction of roles between board members and the district-level administration.

Step Six: At this time, the plan should be made available to stakeholders at the school or district who are not directly involved in the process. This will provide them an opportunity to ask questions for understanding and to make suggestions for improvement. Because the Vision, Mission Values, Goals, and Objectives have already been approved, suggestions and changes should only be made on the *action items*. The planning team reviews all suggestions and includes the recommendations they feel would improve the plan. Once the plan has been completed, it should guide building and district personnel in future professional practice.

JACKSON PUBLIC SCHOOLS STRATEGIC PLAN

On February 11, 2019, the district of Jackson Public Schools (JPS) in Jackson, Mississippi, released a five-year strategic plan (Jackson Public Schools, 2018). This plan is a product of the type of planning process presented by McQueen and Burnham (2015). This plan is not presented and discussed in this book because JPS is a model of success and growth. In fact, the district is struggling with entrenched poor performance and multiple contextual issues common to inner-city school districts serving high minority and low SES student populations across the country. Indeed, while showing strong gains between 2013 and 2019 in National Assessment of Educational Progress (NAEP) scores (see table 3.1), Mississippi struggles with severe underfunding of public schools, the lowest teacher

Table 3.1 Mississippi National Assessment of Educational Progress (NAEP) Scale Score and National Rank Changes 2013–2019

	2013 Miss.	2013 NR*	2015 Miss.	2015 NR*	2017 Miss.	2017 NR*	2019 Miss.	2019 NR*	State Rank Difference 2013–2019**
Fourth Grade Reading	209	49th	214	45th	215	45th	219	30th	Plus 19
Fourth Grade Math	231	50th	234	46th	235	40th	241	19th	Plus 31
Eighth Grade Reading	253	51st	252	51st	256	46th	256	45th	Plus 6
Eighth Grade Math	271	49th	271	46th	271	47th	271	44th	Plus 5

Source: National Center for Educational Statistics, 2019.

Note: * National Rank (NR) includes the District of Columbia and Department of Defense Education Authority for a total of fifty-two jurisdictions.

** Scores include ties (if the rank is nineteenth, this means eighteen states and jurisdictions scored higher).

salaries in the nation, the highest poverty rate in the nation, and a severe teacher shortage. JPS is burdened with an ongoing drop in enrollment, an aging and crumbling infrastructure, a lack of certified teachers, a failing rating, and near takeover by the Mississippi Department of Education. Nonetheless, there are indications of change in JPS with new leadership, new energy, and a new five-year strategic plan. Dr. Errick Greene was appointed superintendent of JPS in August 2018, following service as chief of schools in Tulsa, Oklahoma. He earned his doctorate at the University of Pennsylvania and has school leadership experience in Detroit, Baltimore, Inglewood, California, and he served as principal in Washington, DC. Dr. Green has brought focus and enthusiasm to the district with a new leadership team.

During his first year, JPS's state accountability score (Mississippi Department of Education, 2019) increased by 10 percent from 456 to 504 points and its accountability rating from an "F" to a "D." No one knows how the strategic plan will turn out at the end of five years. Regardless, the plans value here is as an example of a coherent change process based on a strategic planning process in a district facing many difficulties and led by an innovative leadership team. A large cadre of stakeholders was also involved, including, as stated in the plan

> scholars (students), parents, teachers, leaders, and community members to better understand their desires for the future of the district. We carefully reviewed the findings and recommendations in the reports written during the past two years by the Mississippi Department of Education, the Council of the Great City Schools, Insight Education Group, and One Voice. Their findings and recommendations are reflected in this plan. (Jackson Public Schools, 2018, p. 6)

The plan, Excellence for All: The strategic plan for educating Jackson scholars, 2019–2024 (Jackson Public Schools, 2018) begins with stating the district's vision and mission prominently displayed on the first page:

> **Vision:** At Jackson Public Schools, we prepare scholars to achieve globally, to contribute locally, and to be fulfilled individually.
> **Mission:** At Jackson Public Schools, we develop scholars through world-class learning experiences to attain an exceptional knowledge base, critical and relevant skill sets, and the necessary dispositions for great success.

The plan is consistent with the McQueen and Burnham model (2015) in many ways. On the first page is the plan articulates the district's core values developed during the planning process. This part of the document begins with a general statement: "*Core Values: At Jackson Public Schools, we believe in the importance of equity, excellence, growth mindset, relationships, relevance, and positive and respectful cultures.*" This is followed by six specific core values:

1. **Equity**—Our vision of equity, put simply, is "all means all." We ensure equity by celebrating each scholar's individuality, interests, abilities and talents; providing each scholar in each school with equitable access to high-quality instruction, courses, and resources; and holding high expectations for all scholars to graduate college-ready and career-minded. Similarly, we recognize and value the individual abilities, experiences and talents of our staff; providing all staff with equitable access to opportunities for development and growth; and ensuring that such opportunities are provided through clear and transparent processes.
2. **Excellence**—High expectations for our scholars help to prepare them for college and career paths. High expectations from and for all adults foster ownership, consistency, and transparency. Every member of our district performs with an attention to detail and the quality that each task demands in order to achieve great outcomes.
3. **Growth Mindset**—Our leaders—scholars and staff—thrive in environments where belief in their abilities is affirmed. Everyone in the organization embraces the ideal that effort and perseverance lead to success.
4. **Relationships**—It is essential to develop relationships through mutual respect of culture, social context, and community. This allows us to create a community of safety, trust, productive vulnerability, and genuine connection as we celebrate successes and value opportunities for constructive feedback.
5. **Relevance**—Scholars experience relevant education that is engaging, motivating, and inspiring, leading to a lifelong commitment to learning. Our scholars must learn to connect with each other, the larger community, and the 21st-century world, ultimately developing agency to contribute to positive change in Jackson, in Mississippi, and in the world.
6. **Positive and Respectful Culture**—Scholars and staff thrive in learning environments where growth and achievement are the highest priorities and climates are safe, positive, and respectful. These environments engage and excite all scholars, leaving them hungry for more knowledge. All adults contribute to a positive and respectful culture allowing them to experience more productivity, increased retention, and joy at work.

Following the articulation of core values, a personal letter from Dr. Greene is presented to stakeholders affirming a set of five commitments ("A strong start, innovative teaching and learning, talented and empowered work teams, joyful learning environments, and a culture of accountability and excellence") and describing what these commitments mean to scholars, families, staff, and community members. In step two, McQueen and Burnham (2015) tell strategic planners to "come together and reach common agreement on where the school or district is today." The strength of the plan is its transparency regarding the district's performance and challenges expressed in the JPS plan with this story of recent events.

> Jackson, Mississippi—the community we serve—is both the capital city and the state's only urban municipality. Almost 30 percent of the city's population lives in poverty, with the negative impact of these socioeconomic indicators disproportionately affecting the city's African-American residents.
>
> In school years 2015–2016, 2016–2017, and 2017–18, the district received an F rating from the Mississippi Department of Education. And while the number of individual schools receiving a D or F rating has declined from 40 in 2015–16 to 37 in 2017–18, about two-thirds of the district's schools are still drastically underperforming. In 2017–18, nearly a quarter of our scholars were chronically absent, and a growing body of research shows that chronic absenteeism is directly related to lower academic performance.
>
> While our challenge is great, several recent events have converged to make this an opportune time to embark upon a new path. In the fall of 2016, given significant declines in the district's performance on state-mandated assessments, as well as violations of numerous state accreditation standards, the district was placed on probation by the Mississippi Department of Education. The state board of education voted to take over the district in September 2017 and submitted to Governor Bryant a proposed declaration of emergency as required by law.
>
> Rather than carry out the declaration, Governor Bryant consulted Mayor Chokwe Antar Lumumba, the W. K. Kellogg Foundation, and various education experts, to determine a plan that would best serve the Jackson community. The result was the creation of a commission charged with meaningfully engaging the community and conducting a student-centered assessment of Jackson Public Schools that would inform a plan of action for the district. With these goals in mind, the Better Together Commission (BTC) was formed with 15 members appointed by Governor Bryant, Mayor Lumumba, the W. K. Kellogg Foundation, and Jackson Public Schools. Tasked by the BTC, Insight Education Group developed a comprehensive report, *"Ready to Rise: Our Scholars, Our Future, Our Time."* This report included a robust data collection process; review of recent, relevant research; and 51 specific recommendations to help the district chart a course for success.
>
> In October 2018, the Jackson Public Schools Board of Trustees appointed Errick L. Greene, Ed.D. as the new superintendent. His arrival provides a fresh outlook toward helping to mitigate the challenges and recognize the opportunities in our district. A complement of highly talented leaders with expertise in school/district turnaround and teaching and learning was assembled to support Dr. Greene in district transformation efforts.

At this point, the plan has articulated the "core components of the strategic plan: Vision, Mission, and Values" (McQueen & Burnham, 2015). From this, the JPS presents the goals based on expressed values with ten "targeted outcomes" (Jackson Public Schools, 2018, p. 7). The outcomes are presented in three columns: "Where we will be in 2024," "Where we are now," and "How we will measure progress." Table 3.2 presents the ten targeted outcomes. The critical feature of this set of goals is that they are attainable within the five year time frame. JPS is not seeking 100 percent proficiency in five years, which is an unreasonable goal in any district; rather, it is seeking 40 percent proficiency. Nonetheless, if the district reaches its goals, it will experience significant and likely sustainable progress.

Table 3.2 JPS Strategic Plan—Ten Targeted Outcomes

Milestones 2024?	Measurements?	
Where Will We Be in 2024?	Where We Are Now	How Do We Measure Our Progress?
All scholars have access to a high-quality JPS PreK experience	580 available seats	Number of "seats" in PreK
An average of 40% or more JPS scholars performing proficiently (at level 4 or level 5) in Reading and Mathematics across grades 3–8 and High School End of Course exams (English II/Algebra I)	24.7% English/Language Arts; 19.6% Mathematics	MAAP
50% or more scholars performing proficiently (at level 4 or level 5) in Reading and Mathematics by the end of 3rd grade	29.9% English/Language Arts; 21% Mathematics	MAAP
Double the percentage of scholars performing proficiently (at level 4 and level 5) in Reading and Mathematics by the end of 8th grade	16.8% English/Language Arts; 15.8% Mathematics	MAAP
Triple the percentage of scholars performing proficiently in Algebra by the end of 10th Grade (from 10.7% to 30%)	10.7% at level 4 or level 5	MAAP Algebra I 10th Grade
Increase the average composite score on ACT to 21 or above	15.6	ACT
80% or more of JPS scholars graduating in four years	71%	Percentage of scholars enrolled in 9th grade who graduate four years later
10% or fewer of JPS scholars suspended per school year	15%	District discipline data

Milestones 2024?	Measurements?	
Where Will We Be in 2024?	Where We Are Now	How Do We Measure Our Progress?
Decrease chronic absenteeism to no more than 20% of JPS scholars	26%	Attendance data
Parents and families express overall satisfaction with their scholar's school	Baseline to be established in SY 19–20	Comprehensive Needs Assessment Survey

After the presentation of targeted outcomes with embedded goals and objectives, the JPS strategic plan presents Actions Items to accomplish the objectives using the five commitments. Each "Commitment in Action" is followed by a list of key initiatives with an implementation plan. The implementation plan is based on three different processes for each of the five years of implementation: P (Planning), I (Initial Implementation), and R (Continuous Refinement). For example, Commitment #1 is "A Strong Start" (p. 8). See table 3.3, for an example of how the implementation of each "Commitment in Action" is structured.

Similar detail is provided for the remaining of "Commitments in Action." The JPS plan concludes with a description of how the plan will guide administrative action, allocation of resources, and community engagement over the next five years. Responsibility for execution of the plan is led by the superintendent and the central office staff but is also shared with the schools and community stakeholders. The final element in the plan is a "Profile of a JPS Graduate." This profile provides a clear portrait of the vision of the plan in regard to student outcomes.

CONCLUSION

Tying the JPS plan back to HRD, this plan serves as a recruiting device to encourage educators motivated to make a difference to be a part of the transformative process and as a guide for hiring teachers who will support the attainment of the plan's goals. It supports a culture and agenda conducive to effective induction and retention. In addition, the plan provides targeted areas of need to guide professional growth, encourages valid assessment of teaching and learning, and articulates cultural norms supportive of the growth process. Finally, it sets expectations for performance that will allow schools to identify individuals not meeting expectations for targeted mediation and possible removal. Again, while this example is at the level of a large urban

Table 3.3 JPS Implementation Plan Example: Commitment #1: A Strong Start

Commitment #1: A Strong Start Key Initiatives	Implementation Years				
	2019–2020	2020–2021	2021–2022	2022–2023	2023–2024
Develop a robust early literacy campaign	P	P	I	R	R
Expand the number of available PreK seats	I	I	I	R	R
Partner with existing head start, daycare, and early childhood centers in Jackson	I	I	R	R	R
Develop a parent academy	P	I	R	R	R
Implement high quality, developmentally appropriate curriculum	I	I	R	R	R

district, it is a model that is useful at any level. The key is for school leaders to approach critical functions, including school-level HRD, as a comprehensive system requiring detailed planning supported by a clear mission, vision, objectives, and measureable action items. Today, school leaders are able to utilize a plethora of technology to support the data collection, data analyses, information management, and communication necessary for effective HRD. Chapter 4 presents the many types of technology available today to support these needs.

Case Reflection 3

Strategic Planning Audit

Review the strategic planning process and product in a school or school district. Based on the available information, review the planning process and resulting plan, examine existing data, relevant school curricula, school documents, and school policies to gain an understanding of what the strategic plan addresses and noting what is missing and should address. Based on the discussion on developing and using strategic plans, compare this to the information found in the schools or district. Write a short narrative citing both strengths, areas for improvement, and ways the plan aligns with current school programs and activities (in other words, is the plan implemented and followed?).

Prompt Questions:

1. If there is no plan available, how might a strategic plan help the school or district accomplish its goals?

2. Was the plan easy to obtain and readily available to stakeholders? What does the answer to this question tell you about the role and meaning of the plan within the school or district?
3. Are administrators and faculty familiar with the plan and actively working to follow its directives and achieve its goals?
4. Do stakeholders view the plan as a tool for positive change in the school?

Chapter 4

Utilizing Technology with Human Resources

INTRODUCTION

The increasing role of technology within the PreK-12 educational setting in the twenty-first century is profound to say the least. Thus, one might suffice that the question is no longer *if* to use the technology, but rather, *what* technology to use and *how* to best utilize it. With new technology being released at a rapid rate, and on a daily basis, the task to determine what technology to use and how to use it can be daunting. In fact, during the first ten months of 2017 alone, it was reported that $8.15 billion was invested in educational technology (Nataf, 2018).

Thus, as one might imagine, new and improved versions of technology currently utilized within the PreK-12 educational setting are being developed as this book enters the market. Nevertheless, the aim of this chapter is to highlight new and innovative technology as it applies to HRD, and, perhaps more specifically, highlight technology as it applies to items such as the recruiting, interviewing, inducting, assessing, and developing staff. In addition, this chapter presents ideas for how educational technology can help in recruiting for diversity, branding a school, and fostering a positive school culture.

RECRUITING

The ability to successfully recruit the top candidates is invaluable to the process of improving teaching and learning in a school. The issue is some school districts have far more to offer than other districts, in the form of salary, geographical location, perks, and the like. For example, a school or district might be able to offer a competitive salary (as well as an attractive array of additional benefits) and the opportunity to live in a desirable location. Or, a school or district may have less to offer in the form of salary, perks, and geographical location but may have much to offer in the form of the opportunity to make an impact and serve in a district serving a population of low SES students.

Regardless, all schools can improve teacher quality through the use of technology in recruiting. By utilizing technology in a unique and innovative manner, a school can recruit the top candidates from an array of angles. As it applies to recruiting, school leaders can post positions on the Internet, including state and district education webpages, and state and national education organization webpages. This is an excellent place to start. In addition, jobs can be announced and advertised on social media outlets such as Twitter, Facebook, Instagram, and LinkedIn. These efforts are supported by the use of a universal hashtag to connect all of the posts for potential applicants.

When posting on social media, it is important to also include a direct link to apply and include language that makes the position attractive. An example of how social media can make things easy for potential applicants, Instagram now has a "swipe up" feature that allows interested educators to directly link to the application, templates for uploading application materials, information about the school and community, and even promotional videos. This will make a school or district attractive to the younger generation of *digital natives* you are recruiting who will be well aware of and comfortable with these features. Also, effective recruiting will utilize the school district and building webpages. These are great places to get the word out about potential or current openings.

Finally, participation in job fairs and the like for recruiting purposes needs to be promoted through all of the aforementioned outlets. Likewise, live updates from the event can further garner interest. Again, these should be supported by a universal hashtag connecting all of the posts. In the end, current technology, especially in areas of communication via social media, provides an array of creative and innovative opportunities for recruiting high-quality applicants to your school. Schools and districts who are the most innovative with regard to recruitment efforts will likely be the ones who find the best talent.

INTERVIEWING

After the recruiting process is complete, it is time to start the interview process. It was not that long ago that all interviews took place face to face, or at the very least by phone. However, with numerous free video conferencing options, not only can schools recruit far-and-wide, but they can also conduct the initial interviews (and in some cases, second round interviews) with individuals almost anywhere. Of course, numerous schools utilize this technology.

Video conferencing provides schools the opportunity to conduct first and second round interviews without the need for out-of-state and foreign candidates to be face to face. Examples of such technology include Skype, Google Hangout, Zoom, Adobe Connect, and Viber (Viber is excellent for international candidates). Although some of this technology is free, most systems provide extended options and services for paid accounts. Likewise, some schools use FaceTime, which is included with most smartphones.

Nonetheless, this technology will allow you to conduct your initial interviews before a candidate is ever invited to campus. This not only allows candidates from afar to be interviewed, but it also reduces the number of candidates invited to campus for a face-to-face interview. Worth noting, in order to keep the interviews consistent across the board for each potential candidate, all interviews should be conducted via video conferencing, even those that live near your district. This is imperative, just as all the same questions should be asked, the setting should be the same for each candidate. If you do not do so, you may be noncompliant with federal and state laws (National Association of College Employees, n.d.).

Finally, it is wise to pilot the options for video conferencing technology presented. This will allow the interview committee to try out each one and determine which one has the features and options most convenient for the committee to use. In addition, this provides the interview committee members the opportunity to troubleshoot any problems and practice using the technology before the actual interviews begin.

INDUCTING AND RETAINING STAFF

There are numerous technologies that may be utilized during the induction process. These include celebrating your new teachers and introducing them to your stakeholders, including students, staff, parents, and community members. Additionally, technology facilitates retention and effective teaching and learning. First, to build a strong culture it is important to *celebrate everything, and celebrate often.* The HR processes presented in the book are designed to inculcate this mindset.

Essentially, a school should constantly be *telling their story and not letting others tell it for them.* For example, when there are new hires, it is important to celebrate them on the school and district webpages and on all of the social media outlets, newsletters (both in hard copy and electronically), and the like related to the school. This sends the message that the school is excited to have the new teacher join the learning community and the school community wants to celebrate your arrival.

This celebrating often extends to introductions at the first staff meeting at the building level. To improve, in addition to the first staff meeting, new teachers need to be celebrated anywhere and everywhere possible. This makes them feel welcome and symbolizes a sense of excitement upon their arrival as part of the team. New teachers should be introduced at the district opening school year gathering and the first staff meeting at the school. A headshot and a brief bio can be posted on the school and district social media pages with the universal hashtag. It is important to include them in the newsletter (district and building levels) and be sure to include a few sentences about them in the welcome letters to kick off the new academic school year.

As it applies to retaining staff, supportive and effective school leaders need to lead this process. As it applies to effective practice, school leaders should be in every classroom every day. As it applies to this effective practice and the use of technology, school leaders should download the Classroom Walkthrough App. This App can be easily edited to align with the walk-through template required by your respective state and/or district. Second, this App can be utilized from a smartphone or an iPad. Thus, school leaders can easily conduct walk-throughs and provide meaningful and timely feedback to their staff. It is the best practice for leaders to be in every classroom every day (conducting both formal and informal walk-throughs) and to provide timely and meaningful feedback.

By utilizing the Classroom Walkthrough App, a school leader can send their feedback to a respective teachers' inbox before they leave the classroom and head to their next visit. Worth noting here, the visits alone are not enough, school leaders must be able to offer meaningful feedback and do so in a non-punitive manner. Observations, including informal and formal walk-throughs, should not be punitive in nature, rather, this is an opportunity to coach up staff and offer constructive feedback in a positive manner with the underlying goal of doing what is best for students.

This practice improves the trust that teachers have for their administrators. In addition, they feel supported, and they will often go above and beyond the call of duty, and perhaps most importantly, they will choose to stay. When it comes to retaining staff, teachers who feel welcomed, celebrated, and supported, are most likely to stay. Using technology to support induction and monitoring will support efforts to achieve less turnover in your school.

RECRUITING FOR DIVERSITY

In recent years, there has been a push to recruit for diversity in the PreK-12 educational setting. This push is driven by the need to get more individuals who look like the students attending the school in teaching and administrator positions. It goes without saying that teachers and school leaders should reflect the demographics of the student body, not only as it applies to ethnicity but also as it applies to gender.

However, in a majority of schools, this is not the case, and furthermore, many find it difficult to accomplish this task. This ties to the processes to recruit future teachers. For example, only 2 percent of teachers in American public schools are black men (Snyder, de Brey, & Dillow, 2019). This is a troubling statistic indeed. Furthermore, only 23 percent of public school teachers are male—another troubling statistic as it applies to inequality as a majority of school leaders are male (Snyder, de Brey, & Dillow, 2019). Of the more than 13,000 superintendents in the United States, 33 percent are women and 90 percent self-report as white (Tate, 2019).

Nonetheless, recruiting for diversity of teachers in a school starts with school leadership. The first step in increasing teacher diversity is intentionally recruiting minority applicants for teaching positions. Possible avenues include attending teaching job fairs at historically black colleges and universities (HBCU) and taking an assertive stance to interview more minority candidates. In addition, districts should tap future school leaders among current teaching staff that reflect of the student population. Finally, Kozan (2019) outlines the following six steps to hire for diversity:

- Step 1: Conduct a diversity hiring audit on your current hiring process.
- Step 2: Pick one metric to improve for your diversity hiring.
- Step 3: Increase your diversity hiring in your candidate sourcing.
- Step 4: Increase your diversity hiring in your candidate screening.
- Step 5: Increase your diversity hiring in your candidate shortlisting.
- Step 6: Evaluate your diversity hiring metrics.

Kozan (2019) states that "diversity hiring is hiring based on merit with special care taken to ensure procedures are free from biases related to a candidate's age, race, gender, religion, sexual orientation, and other personal characteristics that are unrelated to their job performance."

In the end, schools must make an assertive effort to recruit and hire for diversity in the PreK-12 educational setting. Although there are lower numbers of minorities in the profession itself, it is still plausible with an assertive effort to recruit for diversity in a teaching faculty. A good place to start is on HBCU campuses and campuses that are defined as Hispanic-serving institutions. Simply, the problem of low levels of diversity in the teaching and administrative professions in the United States will be solved when individual schools engage in ongoing intentional efforts to recruit and hire more minority faculty.

BRANDING

Although somewhat new to the PreK-12 educational setting, individual branding and organizational branding have long been part of the business environment. However, with the onslaught of technology, including social media and the use of hashtags, there are increasing efforts by schools and districts, along with individuals serving in school districts, to brand themselves. This is an opportunity for schools to *tell their story*, a critical element in recruiting, which was discussed earlier in this chapter.

A school can effectively enhance its brand through the use of educational technology such as the school's websites, newsletters, e-mail blasts, and social media with a universal hashtag. From an individual basis of teacher or administrator, branding is mainly achieved through the utilization of social media outlets, and personal or professional webpages and blogs. Regardless of the type of branding, effective content focuses on the desired stakeholder perception of a school, a classroom, or an individual educator. The key is what the school community wants stakeholders to think of when they think about the school, a classroom, or an individual educator.

The use of technology for branding creates a digital footprint. This footprint includes all the information (text and imagery) that are retrievable from a Google search and all post connected via a universal hashtag related to the school or individual's brand. Content posted on social media in an effort to brand is a careful dance of exercising humility and bragging, and, depending on the audience reading the content, the audience might not be able to tell the difference. Thus, it is important to be mindful of what is posted and how it is posted. Nonetheless, branding should be done through a lens of telling the school's own story versus letting others tell it for them. The use of social media and web-based technology is an effective tool for rebranding a school in a positive direction. This can mean the chance to rebrand a classroom and give parents a pulse on each school day in a respective class. This can mean the opportunity of branding all of the work a teacher or administrator is doing as an individual, including innovative practices, presentations, conferences, and awards and recognitions.

When it comes to branding, a strong message promotes the dedication and hard work of the professional community and individuals in the school: "We are working hard to accomplish great things and we want you to know about it." When it comes to classrooms and individuals, there are almost unlimited branding opportunities. Remember, start with the end in mind. Ask what the brand should say about the school, the classroom, or the individual. Finally, most districts have policies regarding the creation and use of social media and other technology. All efforts to brand the school or individuals in the school should begin with a careful review of all relevant policies and procedures to ensure full compliance.

SCHOOL CULTURE

Similar to branding, communication technology, including social media outlets, may be used to foster a positive school culture. The things a school celebrates, or does not celebrate, provide a powerful symbolic message. For example, some of the best schools regularly celebrate the good things happening on a day-to-day basis via their websites, social media outlets, e-mails, automated messaging systems, and newsletters.

Whereas, other schools do nothing in the form of celebrating positive activities and accomplishment at all. The difference between these approaches to celebration is schools that celebrate everything and celebrate often are usually schools characterized by a positive culture. Following are some tips on suing utilizing technology to celebrate all of the wonderful things that happen in a school:

- When celebrating items on social media, use the Hootsuite App. The Hootsuite App acts as a dashboard to post on and operate all of a school's or individual's social media. Most importantly, Hootsuite allows the scheduling of posts in advance. For example, a building principal can schedule the promotion and celebration of all the events for the upcoming week. Such events may include a volleyball game Tuesday night, a PTO meeting Wednesday night, a school board meeting on Thursday night, a football game on Friday night, and a Cookie Dough fundraiser on Saturday. By scheduling all of this information to be released in advance, the school leader can focus on posting about the day-to-day events and celebrations throughout the week without worrying about the reminders for the events.
- As it applies to social media and the like, the following outlets for *celebrating everything, and celebrating often* are recommended:
  - Instagram (utilize swipe up feature)
  - Facebook
  - LinkedIn
  - Twitter
  - All with a universal hashtag
  - District/building webpages
  - District/building newsletters
  - Electronic/hard copy newsletters
  - District/building e-mail blasts
  - District/building automatic messaging systems
- Last, but certainly not least, schools should utilize a quality profile report. This is a district-created annual report that highlights all of the wonderful things that happened over the most recent academic school year. This report

includes district financial data, academic achievement, accomplishments of athletic teams, and any other positive news about the school. Essentially, it is the celebration of everything, leaving no stone unturned. In the state of Ohio, almost all school districts utilize a quality profile report. Quality profile reports originated when schools decided they no longer wanted to be known just for their standardized test scores. These schools understood scores were part of their story, but they wanted to share much more with their stakeholders. Again, this profile report tells the entire story of a district from the beginning to the end of the year. While it includes the academic achievement data, it also highlights and celebrates much more. In recent years, a template was created and shared among districts. (An excellent example of a quality profile report exists here [Upper Arlington Schools, 2018]: https://www.uaschools.org/Downloads/quality%20profile%2017-18%20FINAL.pdf.)

CONCLUSION

This chapter presented and discussed several new and innovative opportunities to utilize technology with HRD. These include applications for recruitment, hiring, onboarding, retaining staff, recruiting for diversity, branding, and fostering a positive school culture.

In the twenty-first century, through a continuous growth mindset, it is imperative that schools continuously look for new and improved ways of doing things, not only as it relates to HRD but also as it relates to all processes related to the schoolhouse. This positive orientation to change is, like it or not, becoming a mandate of our profession. As Casas (2018) wrote, "The finest educators consider it professional malpractice to not change when they learn new and better ways of doing their work."

Case Reflection 4
"Look Out Honey, Cause I'm Using Technology"

You are currently serving in a district where 100 percent of your students are on free and reduced lunch. That is, you are serving in a district that serves students who are considered to have low SES. Furthermore, your district has strict policies and procedures when it comes to social media. However, in just your second year as principal, you quickly realize that in meeting with your new hires as part of the ongoing induction process, one of their biggest concerns they have is the inability to connect with and communicate with parents. In addition, several have expressed concerns over the current culture of the school. In an effort to be proactive, you have been actively seeking out and reading an abundance of literature with hopes of mapping out some ideas to address the concerns of your new teachers. After reading an article written by Ungarino (2015) highlighting a Pew Research Center study (Smith, 2015), it was revealed that poorest members of society check their smartphones and social media dozens more times in a single day than the average user. After reading this article, you have an idea of how social media might be the link to communicating with parents throughout your school. In addition, after reading Davis and Fowler's book, you realize that social media may be another way to foster a positive school climate and culture in your district. However, in the same instance, you remember that your district has strict policies and procedures when it comes to social media. Being mindful of this, and given the information presented earlier in the case reflection, and within the chapter, please answer the following questions.

Prompts:

1. What steps would you take to suggest new policy and procedures as it applies to social media use and the like within your school?
2. How would you suggest social media and the like be used by administrators and teaching staff throughout the district in order to communicate with parents, among other stakeholders?
3. How would you suggest social media and the like be used to help better foster a positive school climate and culture in your school
4. How would you share best practices for utilizing social media and the like to communicate with stakeholders (namely parents) and to *celebrate everything, and celebrate often?*
5. What other items might you implement in your district as it applies to better communication with parents as well as fostering a positive school climate and culture?

Section II

HIRING AND RETAINING TEACHERS

Chapter 5

Successfully Recruiting and Hiring Instructional Personnel

INTRODUCTION

There are two primary goals in this chapter. The first is to present and discuss the current best practices in the recruitment and hiring of instructional personnel. The second purpose is to examine these critical HRD practices through the thematic lenses of this book: organizational culture, teaching and learning, economic efficiency and costs, and strategic planning. Before beginning, it needs to be clear that recruiting, selecting, and inducting policies and practices vary considerably from district to district and from school to school.

Many school districts do not encourage individual schools or school-based administrators to recruit, while others allow considerable discretion to school-based personnel regarding recruiting. The same is true for teacher selection and hiring. In some districts, hiring is highly centralized; in others, school-based administrators play a significant role. Many districts also provide extensive new teacher induction programs at the district level and have specific programs in place that all school administrators are expected to follow.

In other districts, induction is the responsibility of individuals working in schools. In most schools, these HRD practices fall somewhere between full district and school-based control. Typically, there is a combination of district policies and involvement combined with school-level influence and flexibility in application. In all situations, however, there is much that school leaders may do to ease the transition into teaching. Recruiting, hiring, and inducting instructional personnel are critical to effective school leadership, administration, and management. The goal is to hire the highest quality instructional personnel available, provide these individuals with what they need to perform at their highest level, and retain them in the organization as satisfied and productive professionals. Effective hiring begins with successful recruiting.

THE RECRUITMENT OF TEACHERS

The goal of recruitment is to receive applications from high quality and highly qualified individuals for each open instructional position in a school or district. The population of quality and qualified instructional personnel potentially willing to work in a school or district at the current salary level constitutes the *supply of teachers* in the labor market. Ideally, it is the job of a school's leadership team to hire the highest quality teachers available in the market.

This is another way of saying that the goal is to recruit in a manner that allows the school to hire personnel, who will provide the highest quality and quantity of instruction available for each dollar it spends on professional instructional services. Recruiting is a process of identifying qualified and available instructional personnel in the market, informing them of open positions, providing information about the school, and encouraging these individuals to apply. Also, individuals will select the option they believe will offer the most benefits among all available choices; thus, it is vital recruiting practices to sell the qualities of a school to job applicants seeking a teaching job. Recruiting is a form of *marketing*.

A successful recruiting process requires careful planning. Planning for recruiting is conducted through/during the SHRP process (see chapter 3). Planners need to intentionally include the recruiting of instructional personnel as part of the comprehensive HR plan. A successfully developed and applied recruiting plan facilitates the strategic goals of the organization. There are three guidelines that will assist in planning for the effective recruitment of teachers. First, *recruit widely*. Schools or districts should recruit in a manner to reach the largest percentage of available instructional personnel in a market. Second, *recruit efficiently*. Recruiting budgets are generally small, making it essential for school leaders to find ways to reach a large number of qualified individuals at a low cost. The Internet is a highly efficient method to recruit. Electronic recruiting options include an array of educational job search websites (some are free, while others require a fee), targeted e-mails, messaging, and tweets, job or educationally relate list serves, and school and individual websites and/or blogs. Third, *recruit ethically*. All schools and districts need to recruit high-quality teachers, and when unethical recruiting practices occur, the entire profession is damaged. Unethical recruiting practices include:

- providing false or misleading information;
- saying or presenting negative comments on other schools or districts;
- targeting and approaching professional practitioners working in other schools and districts (individuals working in other schools/districts may contact another school or district about employee opportunities and is

appropriate to respond; however, it is not ethical to "raid" neighboring schools and districts in an attempt to lure their outstanding personnel); and
- recruiting in a manner that discriminates against any individual on the bases of race, ethnicity, gender, sexual orientation, religious preference, or national origin.

The next stage in the planning process for recruiting is to develop a position announcement.

The *position announcement* is a common description of the position that will consistently appear in all recruiting materials. An effective position announcement specifically describes the job and related responsibilities and qualifications. It must include specific procedures for applicants to follow. People tend to stop reading quickly so it is imperative that the announcement be clear and concise. It is best, when possible, to isolate job descriptions into discrete roles. For example, it is better to post an announcement for a social studies teacher and another announcement for a head football coach, rather than an announcement for a football coach and social studies teacher. Of course, a school may not have the flexibility to offer any alternatives to this specific combination of jobs, and it would be misleading to encourage individuals to apply for a position as a social studies teacher, when the job also requires skills and experience in football coaching.

However, the goal should be to hire the most qualified social studies teacher for teaching history and the best coach for coaching football and only combine the two positions if an individual is the most qualified applicant for both roles. The job announcement also needs to provide a short and attractive description of the school or district. After all, the hope is that the person who is hired makes a long-term commitment to the community. Finally, the date that the search will close and the date when a decision will be made also need to be included in an effective announcement. The position announcement, however, is only one part of a comprehensive recruiting (marketing) strategy.

A key element to successful recruiting is the marketing of a school or district to potential employees. Thus, it is critical during the planning process to identify what makes the school a good place to work. What is special or unique about the school? What is special or unique about the community? It is not enough to identify the positive attributes of the school. The planning process must also specifically determine how the positive message is going to be presented and reinforced (see chapter 4).

The final stage in the recruiting planning/recruiting processes is the development of strategies for effectively sending the desired message to the maximum number of potential applicants. There are multiple means to advertise open instructional positions. The value of using the Internet as a recruiting tool was previously discussed. Another option for low-cost recruiting includes educational job fairs. Job fairs provide access to a large number of potential teachers; however, the large numbers of schools and/or districts commonly attending job fairs make it difficult for one school to differentiate itself from other schools. Internal recruiting is a great place to start and many positions, especially administrative, are filled by personnel within the school or district.

Many schools recruit outstanding student teachers or interns who are doing their fieldwork at the school. Many positions are filled from referrals from current staff. With referrals, however, there is a danger of conflict of interest and other internal political concerns. Placement offices at local colleges and universities along with placement services of professional organizations are usually free of charge and should always receive position announcements. Target letters or e-mails are also effective, depending on the source and quality of the target lists. Placing advertisements in newspapers and/or in professional magazines and journals is also an option; however, published advertisements are expensive and often fail to reach the most qualified applicants.

Published advertisements often result in high number of applications from unqualified (uncertified) individuals. Finally, there are search firms and consultants available and these may be effective in locating and recruiting highly skilled individuals, especially in other sectors of the economy or in other regional markets. Using search consultants, however, is highly expensive.

As in all HR planning and practices, it is important to estimate costs (monetary costs, time requirements, and opportunity costs) and compare those costs to expected benefits. Table 5.1 provides a guide for advertising/marketing options and general levels of costs and expected benefits.

Table 5.1 Advertising Options for Instructional Positions in a School

Advertising Method	Monetary Cost	Time Cost	Effectiveness
Educational Job Fairs	Low	Medium/High	Medium
Paid Education Job Websites	Medium	Low	Medium/High
Paid General Job Websites	Low/Medium	Low	Low
Free Education Job Websites	Low	Low	Medium
Free General Job Websites	Low	Low	Low
School/District Home Pages, Blogs, and Websites	Low/Medium	Medium	Medium
Internal Recruiting (Including Interns and Student Teachers)	Low	Medium	Medium
Staff Referrals	Low	Low	Low/Medium
College and University Placement Offices	Low/Medium	Low/Medium	Medium/High
Professional Organization Placement Services	Low	Low	Low/Medium

Advertising Method	Monetary Cost	Time Cost	Effectiveness
Targeted Letters and E-mails	Low/Medium	Medium/High	Medium
Newspaper Advertisements	Medium/High	Low	Low/Medium
Professional Magazine/Journal Advertisements	High	Low	Low
Search Firms and Consultants	Very High	Low/Medium	High

In summary, effective recruiting for instructional personnel is well planned. The recruiting process needs to reach the target audience, be efficient, and be ethical. A well-crafted position statement and a comprehensive marketing strategy should emphasize the strengths of the school. There must be a clear plan for advertising any teaching position. Whether at the school or district level, recruiting is critical to hiring the best possible instructional personnel. Nonetheless, it is only the beginning of the hiring process.

THE SELECTION AND HIRING OF INSTRUCTIONAL PERSONNEL

It is important to remember that hiring a teacher is an economic process. Just like when you go to the store, you are purchasing something; in the case of teacher hiring, you are purchasing the professional services of a teacher. Like any purchase, the goal is to get the highest quality of product/service at a given price. On the other hand, all individuals selling their professional services will make choices based on what they believe is the best option available to them.

There are two parts that factor into the decision of a person a school wants to hire. First, the availability of other opportunities (teaching in other districts or other schools and the demand for a person's skills in other professions). Second, the attractiveness of a specific professional context in terms of intrinsic (personal values, moral purpose, love of teaching, and desire to make a difference) and extrinsic (community and neighborhood characteristics, reputation of the school, working conditions, salary, and benefits) characteristics have a major influence on an individual's choice.

This section presents the key issues and elements of the hiring process for purposes of both planning and implementation. Thus, this information may be used to assist planning and to guide practice. For the building-level administrator, hiring practices must be consistent with district policies and practices. While district policies and practices vary significantly, principals must follow them, nonetheless. In addition, when principals make hiring decision in isolation by themselves, there are implications for induction and the overall health of the organizational culture.

The hiring process, first, is an *assessment process*. The goal of the organization is to assess the quality, qualifications, and fit of each applicant. Scriven (1990) provides a useful framework for assessing applicants for instructional positions in schools. Scriven defines two areas for assessment: *merit* and *worth*. Merit refers to the professional skills, or the extent to which the individual applicant measures up to the accepted standards of the teaching profession, especially in the area(s) for which a position is being advertised. Merit is any quality that will have an impact on student learning. It is, in many forms, the applicant's ability to teach.

Merit is the key determining criteria in hiring decisions. Worth is the value of an employee to the institution, which arises from considerations other than their ability to perform their duties. By its definition, worth raises ethical and legal questions. Worth incorporates many things, including attitude, motivation, level of cooperation, appearance, political factors (it is not ethical to consider political influences as a factor in selection decisions but it is nonetheless true that hiring certain individuals may provide political benefits to a school—unfortunately, it is a practice in some schools and districts with poor hiring practices), gender, racial, and ethnic background. In most situations, worth is not an acceptable criterion for the assessment of applicants. In some cases, however, it is appropriate to consider the gender, race, and ethnicity of an applicant for the purpose of increasing diversity in an organization.

For example, it would be appropriate to consider the "worth" of a Hispanic applicant for a position in a school with a large Hispanic population and no Hispanic teachers. A recent Supreme Court decision *Schuette v Coalition to Defend Affirmative Action* (2014) prohibits institutions to establish *racial quotas* for the selection of students, but racial quotas may still be established for selection of educational personnel. While establishing quotas typically involves a complex set of politically sensitive decisions, quotas may be useful in balancing the racial characteristics of school faculties and the students.

Scriven provides a simple guideline for using merit and worth: hiring decisions should be based on merit, and only when two or more applicants are assessed with equal merit should worth ever be considered. Therefore, the key factor for leadership is the ability of the individuals participating in the hiring process to accurately assess the merit of each applicant. There are eight sources of data commonly available to assess the qualifications of applicants in selecting teachers for employment:

1. Application form
2. Writing samples (letters of interest, applications essays, and/or academic work)

3. Records of teaching (student teaching assessments or previous teaching evaluations)
4. Academic record (degrees, institutions, GPAs, Praxis Scores)
5. Professional references
6. Interviews
7. Demonstrations of teaching (actual opportunities to teach a lesson, or portfolios)
8. Evidence of student growth in past teaching assignments

These sources of data are used to assess an applicant's classroom teaching skill, content knowledge and expertise, knowledge and skill in monitoring and assessing student learning, written and oral communication skills, personal relations and responsibility (professionalism), technology skills, organizational and planning skills, and out-of-class contributions (noninstructional).

According to Scriven (1990), several factors that should not be considered when selecting teachers for employment include an applicant's personal or family life, appearance, personality, teaching style, race, gender, religion, or age. This requires a delicate balancing act because an applicant characteristics, such as personality or teaching style, may have an influence on teaching effectiveness. In other words, these variables may be an indication of merit. Further, the race and gender of an applicant may be appropriate for consideration in places where diversity of teaching faculty is needed.

On the other hand, a wide variety of teaching methods has been shown to be effective and there are extremely effective teachers with different personality traits (happy, grumpy, outgoing, and even reserved). Given this, it is the ethical responsibility of individuals participating in a search and selection process to focus, as much as the data will allow, on the applicant's effectiveness with children through the teaching and learning process. In other words, the focus should be on results or potential pedagogical effectiveness of the applicant.

Well-planned and implemented hiring policies, procedures, and processes improve the ability to accurately assess the merit of each candidate. As a general rule, one or two individuals are not able to effectively assess the merit of an entire pool of applicants. Effective and accurate assessment of applicants requires a group effort typically in the form of a *selection committee*. Effective and accurate assessment is also expensive, especially in time cost; however, the benefits of selecting and hiring the best teacher available are extremely valuable.

Selection committees vary in size and representation. The optimal size is a balance between a committee that is too small, resulting in a high workload and a limited number of voices, and a committee that is too large, resulting in difficulties in scheduling meetings and reaching a group consensus. Most committees have between five and ten members.

Allowing stakeholder groups (teachers, parents, community members, and support staff) to select representatives for the committee facilitates a valuable sense of ownership and involvement in the school's organizational culture. This also dramatically increases the acceptance of new personnel into the school. The principal can maintain control of a committee by selecting the members, but there may be a loss of the benefits from having multiple representatives. Group representatives selected by the principal will not be as likely to be viewed by stakeholders as representing their interests. It is wise for the principal to place one or two administrators on the committee and select a trusted individual as chair.

Another option is to allow the committee to select its own chair, but this may result in less influence from the principal. One of the most important factors to a successful committee process is for the committee to be *charged* with clear expectations of behavior and conduct, policies and procedures, meeting times, deadlines, and specific deliverables. The charging of a committee is typically the responsibility of the principal. In almost every case, the deliverable of a selection committee is to make a recommendation to a single decision-making authority, usually the principal.

These recommendations come in many forms, including a list of top three applicants (may or may not be rank-ordered) or a single individual. Depending on the number of applicants, the work of the search committee may be significantly reduced through a preliminary screening process. Preliminary screening is used to eliminate applicants, who do not meet predetermined standards or criteria, or to identify a percentage of top applicants (e.g., top 50 percent). The goal is to select a pool of potential applicants for further comprehensive assessment. In most cases, preliminary screening selects applicants for interview.

The data used for preliminary screening are contained in the application materials and there should be no contact of references during the preliminary screening. Thus, prescreening is based on writing samples, records of teaching, and academic records. Often, prescreening may occur at more than one level. Staff members may be used to eliminate applicants who do not meet the minimal requirements, but these decisions should be reviewed. If needed, an administrator, a subcommittee (three members), or the chair of the search committee may further prescreen applications. Table 5.2 provides a guide for assessment of applicants during prescreening, interviews, and final recommendation.

It is necessary to have a system in place for assessing and comparing applications in an equitable and ethical manner. This process is typically conducted through a common scoring system. A 1–3 scale is easiest to use. All items used for consideration in selection are converted to the common score. Quantitative scores are converted through a simple conversion scale.

Table 5.2 Prescreening Applicants for Instructional Positions

Data Source	Types	Description	Skills Assessed	Data Analyses	Value
Application Form	Application	Applicant information, background, education, experience, service contributions, references	All, but at a very general level	Contains content that is assessed at other levels	
Writing Sample	Letter of Introduction	The letter the applicant attached to their application introducing themselves and expressing a desire to work in the school	Communication	Not appropriate for formal evaluation	Low
	Required Essay for Application	The applicant is requested to write a response to an essay question as part of the submitted application	Communication Professionalism	Rubric	Medium
	Sample of Academic Writing	The applicant is requested to produce an academic paper from their undergraduate or graduate studies	Communication Content knowledge	Rubric	Low/Medium
Records of Teaching	Portfolio	The applicant is asked to produce a professional or student teaching portfolio	All	Rubric	Medium/High
	Student Teaching Evaluation	The applicant is asked to provide a copy of evaluations of their student teaching	Pedagogy (performance) Content knowledge Assessment Organization Professionalism Planning Technology	Rubric	Medium/High
	Teaching Evaluations	The applicant is asked to provide a copy of evaluations from their teaching experience	All	Rubric	Medium/High

(Continued)

Table 5.2 (Continued)

Data Source	Types	Description	Skills Assessed	Data Analyses	Value
	Evidence of Past Student Growth (Bates)	The applicant is asked to provide measured data to evidence past student growth (if available)	All	Matrix	High
Academic Record	Degrees		Pedagogy (knowledge) Content knowledge Communication	Certification Content area	Medium
	Coursework		Pedagogy (knowledge) Content knowledge	Content area	Medium
	GPA		Pedagogical knowledge Content knowledge Communication	Scale	Medium
	Praxis Scores		Pedagogical knowledge Content knowledge	Scale	Medium

For example, GPAs may be converted as 0.0–2.75 (unacceptable), 2.76–3.2 (1 point), 3.21–3.6 (2 points), or 3.61–4.0 (3 points).

Rubrics are an effective tool for rating narrative or other forms of qualitative data such as portfolios, essays, writing samples, interviews, and recommendations. Rubrics include a list of the following specific topics or categories for assessment: a clear definition of each category, a rating scale (usually 1–3), and clear description of what each rating means in each category. Scores in individual categories are averaged for a total score on the item. A problem with this method is that different sources of data do not provide the same level of information regarding an applicant's merit. A portfolio may provide much more information than an application essay. The solution to this problem is to establish a multiplier for each source of assessment data. A composite score can then be used to compare applicants. Table 5.3 provides an example of a scaled total score for an applicant.

The total scores of each applicant are compared for decision-making purposes. There are several limitations to this type of process in need of stating. First, a scoring process of any type should be used as a guide and *not the sole criteria for making selection decisions*. Many of the ratings and scores are subjective determinations and may be based on unequal, biased, or invalid data.

There are also many intangible variables and characteristics of applicants that may influence an applicant's teaching ability and fit and these may not be adequately captured through rubrics and/or numerical scores. Many letters, essays, portfolios, and other types of materials prepared by the applicant may contain *unverifiable information*. A common example of unverifiable information is the response to the question: "What is your philosophy of teaching?" Most applicants know the acceptable answer to this question and

Table 5.3 Example Scaled Total Score for Instructional Applicant

Data Source	Scale	Multiplier	Range	Rating	Score
Essay**	1–3	1	1–3	2.1	2.1
Professional Experience*	1–3	1	1–3	2	4
Portfolio**	1–3	3	3–9	2.6	7.8
Teaching Evaluations**	1–3	3	3–9	2.8	8.4
GPA*	1–3	2	2–6	3	6
Praxis Scores*	1–3	1	1–3	3	3
References***	1–3	2	2–6	2.1	4.2
Interview***	1–3	4	4–12	2.6	10.4
Evidence of Student Growth***	1–3	4	4–12	2.8	11.2
Total			21–63		55.1

Notes: * Used for prescreening by the administrative assistant.
**Used for prescreening by the principal and selection subcommittee.
***Used for consideration by the selection committee.

will say what they believe the people making the selection will want to hear: "All children can learn." The response is rarely an indication of merit. References may also be a problem as applicants tend to select references they know will provide a positive recommendation. In addition, many educational professionals are reluctant to provide negative information in order to prevent possible lawsuits.

Often times, recommendations will only confirm that an applicant worked at a school during a specific set of dates. Regardless, *references and former school-based employers* should always be contacted. As a result, assessment rubrics and scores should only be used as a guide to assist a selection committee in using their professional judgment to make the best overall recommendation possible. Although there are many sources of data available to assess applicants, interviews are the most effective and beneficial source of data to choose applicants to offer a position.

Interviews provide an opportunity for individuals involved in the selection process to meet, get to know, and personally assess the top applicants for a position. The interview process needs to be designed so it not only supports the selection of the best applicant but also encourages the best applicant to want to work in your school. The optimal interview process *makes the meeting a special and important occasion*. Interviews need to occur at or near the end of the selection process. Before the top applicants are selected for an interview, the first step is to determine the number of interviewees. This may be predetermined or may also be based on the time available to conduct the interviews or on the number of highly viable applicants in the pool.

If there is a final decision-making authority external to the search committee, this person should be included in the interview or provided an opportunity to individually meet with the applicant. Specific details of the interview process are determined in advance. The first step is a determination of the form of the interview process. Options for the interview include a range from conversational to highly structured. A conversational format provides a more relaxed atmosphere and allows applicants to express their personalities and favorably present their strongest attributes.

Nonetheless, conversational formats are risky and may not flow well, and they are not well suited for making comparisons between applicants. If a conversational format is used, it is important that all applicants interviewed have a similar experience and the prompts are the same. According to the National Association of College Employees (n.d.): "Employers must ensure that all applicants are asked the same or similar questions, and should train its interviewers thoroughly regarding the interview process." Highly structured interviews provide a template for ensuring that the questions cover all desired qualifications and provide a fair and efficient means to compare the responses of each applicant.

Applicants being interviewed should always be provided an opportunity to ask questions of the committee and provide additional information on qualifications to the committee. Regardless of the style used, it is important that everyone involved in the interview process adequately prepare for the interview. Individuals conducting interviews need to participate in either a preparation meeting or more a formal *interviewer training*. Important topics for an interview preparation meeting include:

- how to make the applicant feel welcome, comfortable, and relaxed;
- how to present the school as a good place to work;
- the preparation and overview of the list of questions or topics and clear instructions of the types of questions not to ask;
- the determination and planning for who will speak and when;
- a discussion of procedural issues;
- an overview of what to look for during the interview;
- a presentation of how the interview will end and the applicant thanked and dismissed;
- a determination of who will show them out and how;
- an overview of how each applicant will be assessed during and after the interview; and
- a rehearsal or mock interview.

It is proper to tell applicants when a decision will be made and when they will be contacted. It is unethical and unprofessional practice to fail to contact applicants who are not selected. In addition, doing this may cost you the opportunity to hire a highly qualified individual who was not selected but may be a top applicant in future searchers.

Interviews are an ideal opportunity to assess many of the intangible elements of effective teaching. These include the applicant's ability to explain matters clearly, ability to cope with questions under a high-pressure situation, familiarity with important current issues in education, knowledge of the school and school culture, and teaching-related intellectual and social qualities. After the final applicant is interviewed, the selection process needs to conclude as soon as possible.

CONCLUSION

The decision-making process for final selections needs to be clarified in advance. A common practice is for the committee to rank-order the top three applicants with the principal exercising veto power over the top applicant and having the option of selecting the second or third candidate. Regardless, the better the process is planned and executed, the less likely there will be the need for a principal veto. A consensus or unanimous committee decision is almost never overturned. It is also imperative that the selection committee be prepared in the event the top applicant(s) declines an offer. Once an offer of employment has been accepted and approved, all applicants should be notified by mail. Finally, once an applicant accepts an offer of employment, the next step is the successful induction of the newly hired professional into the school's culture.

Case Reflection 5

Post-Interview Surprise

This reflection is a problem-solving activity designed to simulate the impact on a school's culture and climate of tensions between an administrator's personal values, organizational values, and community values.

You are a leader of a small (400–500 students), diverse, rural high school. The school board and the local community are generally conservative in nature. Words often used to describe the philosophical views of most school board and community members include traditional, fundamentalist, and old school.

Each situation should be considered separately as an individual case.

Under your strategic plan, your highest priority is to improve the instructional quality and teacher quality at your school. You are searching for a new teacher and you have looked at a promising resume for a potential high school teacher. The applicant has been selected for an interview because of strong evidence of highly effective teaching. Following a successful interview, you call the applicant's former principal as a final check prior to offering the applicant a teaching position. If for any reason you decide not to hire the applicant, you have been advised by your district's attorney that you are not required to state the reason why an individual was not selected for employment. Thus, if you decide not to hire the applicant, you do not need to state a reason. During the conversation with the applicant's current principal, without invitation, the principal tells you that the person is a wonderful teacher and that his or her on-the-job behavior is always a model of professional standards; then, the principal says: "There is, however, one thing that I think you should be aware of:

Situation One—Mr. Gunny runs his classroom like a Marine Corps boot camp. His students are required to sit upright, keep their mouths shut, and pay attention. I have received many complaints from parents about his teaching style. Parents are particularly concerned with Mr. Gunny's requirement that all students sit at attention and speak only when spoken to. One parent said, 'he treats my child like a slave.'"

Situation Two—Mr. Youngcoach married our former head cheerleader two days following her high school graduation last May. Although the father was extremely upset, the young woman was eighteen years old and Mr. Youngcoach was twenty-two, and there was no previous indication of an improper relationship prior to the wedding."

Situation Three—Ms. Spindancer is somewhat a hippy. Some parents have complained about the 'satanic' images evident on some of the Grateful Dead stickers on her Volkswagen. Last summer, Ms. Spindancer traveled to Tennessee and attended a music festival called Bonaroo where two teenagers died of drug overdoses. In addition, every spring, Ms. Spindancer takes several days off for religious purposes to attend something called the 'Rainbow Gathering.' Lately, I have heard her telling colleagues that she is planning a trip to Nevada to attend an event called the Burning Man Festival. It is rumored that marijuana and psychedelic drugs are openly used at all these events although there is no indication that Ms. Spindancer partakes."

Situation Four—Mr. Redbone drives a pickup truck with a confederate flag license plate on the front. While this has upset many students and parents, Mr. Redbone refuses to remove the symbolic plate claiming that his having it on his truck is not an attempt to make a racial statement, but, rather, he feels it is an expression of his cultural heritage."

Each Situation Should Be Considered Separately

Prompts:

These cases present ethical dilemmas that might be viewed as a conflict between individual teacher's rights to private lives outside of their profession and the impact of their private lives on the school and community. Place yourself in the position of considering these individuals as potential colleagues and employees in your school.

There are several questions that should be considered:

1. How might a positive decision impact the internal culture of the school?
2. How might a positive decision impact the relationship between the school and its community?

3. Is it appropriate based on the criteria of *merit* and *worth* to consider these types of behaviors in making a hiring decision (and is it ethical, and is it legal)?

Write a brief explanation for each decision. Begin by stating why you would support or not support hiring the individual applicant. Follow with two to three sentences explaining your decision (each applicant is a separate decision and you are not choosing one over another. Thus, you will have four short responses). You may cite personal values, community values, legal issues, ethical issues, or lack of fit in the school; however, remember each applicant rose to the top of your applicant pool based on your assessment of *merit*.

Chapter 6

New Teacher Induction and Mentoring

New teacher induction is "the bridge from initial teacher training to effective instructional practice" (Bubb, Early, & Totterdell, 2005, p. 259). The focus of new teacher induction is on two central goals: the retention and the improvement of new instructional personnel. *The most critical element of successful new teacher induction has nothing to do with programs, policies, and practices; rather, it is a reflection of the school's culture.* If you are an educator, think back to your first year in the profession and how you felt beginning your first teaching job and entering a school. Typically, individual experiences tend toward one of two extremes. Following in Case Reflection 6 are two stories to illustrate the power of the organizational culture in making new teacher induction successful.

Case Reflection 6

New Teacher Induction

Story 1: A brand new teacher arrives at her new school and the people in the school help her to feel valued and appreciated. The school has a "welcoming ceremony" for her and the two other new teachers. During the ceremony, the principal describes her outstanding qualifications and presents the new teacher an engraved name plate to place on her desk and each member of the faculty greets her personally and welcomes her. She knows she can make mistakes and talk to people about problems which she faces in the classroom. She trusts her colleagues and feels comfortable taking risks in her teaching and trying different techniques she learned in college.

Her colleagues are interested in her ideas about teaching. She believes she will be provided everything she needs to be successful. She can see that the assignments of classrooms, courses, students, and duties are conducted in a fair and equitable manner. In fact, as is the case with all new teachers in her school, she is provided an extra planning period each day and no duty assignments during her first year. While she is concerned about teaching U.S. History and A.P. World History, her degree in history provides her with high efficacy in her ability to teach these subjects. She is confident when she has problems with students or parents, her voice will be heard. She's treated as a professional, and if appropriate, is supported by her colleagues and the administration. She has been thoroughly taught the rules and procedures of the organization and knows procedural questions will be answered.

The principal and AP always seem to be around and their doors are always open. When she knocks or sees the administrators, they always smile, greet her, and seem glad to see her. When she speaks to them, they stop what they are doing and give her their full attention. A mentor is assigned to her whom she likes, trusts, and works well with. She is provided frequent opportunities to observe the mentor and other teachers, and the mentor and other teachers observe her. The feedback she receives from her mentor and other teachers is supportive, helpful, and formative. She does not feel like she is being judged.

She is invited to collaborate and team-teach with other teachers. She is offered the opportunity to coach or sponsor extracurricular activities but is not pressured to do so. While she feels her first year will be a challenge full of growth and change, she also feels confident she will do well, and she has a promising future in a teaching career she enjoys. She is glad she decided to major in education and become a teacher. She knows she will make a difference in the lives of many children.

Story 2: A brand new teacher arrives at her new school and is frustrated because people keep mistaking her for a student. A week later, following her introduction at a faculty meeting, she hears coaches at the back table taking bets on whether she will make it through the first full week of classes. The "new teacher" meeting seems to focus mostly on consequences for not doing things correctly (teaching the prescribe curriculum in the proper manner, staying on the curriculum schedule, following the attendance policy, maintaining control of the classroom, and avoiding "too many" discipline referrals).

During the second week, a student disobeyed rules by using profanity and she wrote her first referral. The same afternoon, an AP came to talk to her about the way she treats students and told her that she was expected to resolve these types of discipline issues in the classroom with the students first, parents second, and only as a last resort, should the administration be involved. The student was sent back to class with the admonition to not do it again. She is not sure who she can trust and is fearful of showing any weakness in the classroom.

She is afraid to take any chances but is often uncertain of what she should be doing. Her "classroom" is the last one in a long line of portable buildings. For some reason (she later learned the portable classroom had been left unlocked during the last day of school the following spring and some teachers had gone in and found a few things they needed) the room has no filing cabinets, her desk has two drawers that will not open, the students' desks are a mismatch of sizes and shapes with many of them broken and most of them full of carvings and graffiti, her textbooks are between eight and twelve years old and there are no complete sets, and the clock doesn't work.

She has four preps (World Geography, Civics, Free Enterprise, and one section of Earth Science). She figures the principal must not have noticed her "D" in geology and wonders how she will ever teach Earth Science, a subject she knows little about. Two of her World Geography sections and her Earth Science class are made up entirely of students who failed the class the previous year, and her Civics class has thirty-six students registered (she is told there are several students in the class who really do not come to school much and several others are on their last chance with discipline and will likely not make it through the first month of school). Her daily duty assignment is from 7:00 a.m. to 7:50 a.m. in the student parking lot and she is surprised to discover she is the only adult in the parking lot. The other assigned teacher came out one morning and told her that the new teachers were expected to "keep an eye on things" and she had already done her fair share of "dark mornings in the cold," but, in a couple of years, there would be incoming rookies to take her place.

She was also advised to "keep her cell phone handy" because "lots of things go on in the parking lot." It was made clear to her that favorable duty assignments, classrooms, course assignments, and even students were something teachers "earned" through seniority at the school and by supporting the administration. She was provided a "Teacher Handbook" but many of the procedures were unclear and when she asked an AP for clarification, she was told to read it more carefully. Her mentor seemed nice at first, but lately she seems to be avoiding her. A month ago, the principal notified her he was going to come and observe sometime in the next "week or so" and she should be ready. She recalled her friend from college who got placed on an improvement plan following his first observation by a principal. He has not yet observed her. On top of that, during her interview with the principal, he made it clear he would only hire her if she agreed to coach the women's cross-country track team along with serving as the assistant women's softball coach (at least she had experience playing softball).

While she is enjoying the kids on the cross-country team, practices are keeping her at school until 6:00 p.m. and the Saturday races are taking much of her free time. All in all, she is not sure if she is going through some type of trial by fire, boot camp, or ritualized initiation. At times, she is not sure if she wants to make it through the first year and she wonders why she ever thought she would enjoy a teaching career.

Prompts:

1. In what ways does the culture of the school impact what a new teacher experiences during the first two years in a school?
2. What are some steps a school leader might take to make the experience of newly hired teachers positive?
3. What role do professional teachers have in making the experience of newly hired teachers positive?
4. Is an investment in supporting and meeting the needs of new teachers a wise use of the scarce school resources of time and money? Why or why not?

Originally, the two stories were exaggerated to present each as an extreme example of effective and ineffective new teacher inductions. Over the past twenty years, however, a large number of graduate students report: "Part of Story 2 is my story!" This is a sad commentary but, nonetheless, across schools and districts there are wide variations in the type and quality of the induction services new teachers receive. While many schools have good induction practices, it is rare for there to be an intentional focus on the cultural dynamics of successful induction.

First, an effective new teacher induction program is a wise utilization of available resources. The key caveat is effective. An induction program unable to retain and improve promising teachers is wasteful. Effective new teacher induction is expensive, but the potential benefits extend far beyond new teachers. Simply, effective new teacher induction facilitates and supports a collegial and cooperative organizational culture. Dangel (2006) and Peterson (1995) have developed a broad overview of research on new teacher induction. Here is a list of key elements followed by a description and explanation of each *component of an effective new teacher induction program:*

1. Well planned
2. Early start
3. Introductions
4. Early meetings
5. Assignments
6. Quality mentors
7. Mentor training
8. Mentor fit
9. Assessment of needs
10. Observation and collaboration
11. Consistent and ongoing

As is the case with all HR management activities, careful planning is essential for successful new teacher induction. A *well-planned* induction process includes details of all intentional activities to be used to successfully bring the new person into the organization. Induction planning is also part of the SHRP process. A successful new teacher induction plan includes a description of activities and processes, a timeline, a determination of responsibilities, and a budget. The budget includes monetary costs and personnel time costs. The importance of an *early start* cannot be overstated.

New teacher induction should begin the moment a new teacher is selected and accepts the position. The first step is to provide clear information to the new teacher regarding teaching assignments, preps, and room assignments. It is valuable to explain the induction procedures. New teachers need to be told key dates and exactly what is expected when they begin working. In addition, mentors are much more effective when they are assigned and begin communication with the new teacher early. One of the most helpful things a mentor can do to help a new teacher get off to a good start is to help them prepare their classroom.

Once the school year begins and the teachers arrive, the manner in which a new teacher is introduced to a school is an important moment in a school's symbolic and ritual life. The moment of *introduction* is full of meaning for the new and returning teachers. Simply, how a new teacher is introduced is a symbolic indication of what the new person means to the organization. An ideal, formal introduction is ceremonial and presented as a big moment in the cultural life of the school. It is an opportunity to reinforce and promote the core values and vision of the school.

There should be time for everyone to individually greet and welcome the new teacher. The goal is to present a message to the new teacher: "We welcome you to our school family, we are thrilled to have you, we know you will be successful because we are successful, we are going to provide you with what you need, and we are looking forward to working with you." In addition to meetings typically held by districts for new teachers, schools should also schedule a series of *early meetings* for all new teachers. These meetings should cover school policies, processes, and procedures. They also reinforce the values and vision of the school. Regardless, there is a need for balance here in order to ensure new teachers are not overwhelmed with excessive meetings at the critical time of the beginning of the school year. The key is to schedule a few brief and informative meetings to help monitor and support new teachers by answering questions and providing timely information.

Becoming a teacher should not be a form of ritualized hazing. The types of teaching, duties, and other *assignments* that new teachers are provided have a large influence on the type of experience new teachers encounter. While it is not always possible to provide new teachers reduced duty assignments or teaching loads, new teachers should never be given unfavorable duties, teaching assignments, or classroom assignments.

When the new teacher reports to school, it is the administration's responsibility to ensure the new teachers have everything they need in regard to a clean work space, which should be ready with appropriate furniture, technology, supplies, curriculum materials, and textbooks. One of the most important factors to the experience is the assignment of a *quality mentor*. Individual mentoring is the single most influential factor of a successful induction program. Because mentoring is teaching, the most effective teachers usually, but not always, provide the most effective mentoring. Marginal teachers are rarely good mentors. It is also essential that the mentors be willing, committed, and highly motivated to dedicate significant time to provide support, coaching, and guidance.

Mentoring is extremely time-consuming, and mentors earn and deserve to be compensated for the time and effort the role requires. If monetary compensation is not available (it usually is not), release time may be provided. Mentoring programs, in which the mentors are not compensated, are rarely successful because the normal job duties tend to build during the year, and their availability for mentoring decreases. *Mentor training* is an effective tool to ensure quality mentoring. School-based mentor training is necessary for many reasons. First, it emphasizes the importance of the mentoring process. It provides an opportunity to review the entire induction program. Mentors need to be trained on classroom observation and assessment, identifying strengths and weaknesses, and working with new teachers. Successful mentors are aware of the many challenges faced by new teachers, and they are skilled with providing a wide range of supports.

In addition to being well trained, there also needs to be a good *mentor fit* between the mentor and the new teacher. Successful mentoring depends on the relationship between the mentor and mentee. The relationship needs to be close, trusting, supporting, and collegial. The best way to ensure a good fit is to provide opportunities for mentors to meet new teachers and allow both parties a say in the selection process. In addition, effective mentoring programs, the close relationships required for success, allow for a change of mentors if the relationship is not working for either the mentee or the mentor.

Almost all new teachers have gaps in their abilities and in areas which need improvement. Yet all new teachers do not have the same needs. Thus, it is important to *assess the needs of new teachers*. Peterson (1995) identifies several common needs that new teachers have, namely, pupil assessment, planning skills, organizational skills, ability to motivate students, classroom management, dealing with individual differences, working with parents, utilization of materials, and dealing with student problems.

Some new teachers have problems with classroom management and others may have strong management skills. An effective induction program has an intentional and ongoing plan to assess the needs of new teachers. The mentor is the center of the process but is not the only participant. In fact, formative assessment of a new teacher needs requires a team effort. The process is one of both *observation and collaboration*. The mentor must engage in frequent observation and provide feedback to the teacher, and, in turn, the new teacher should be provided multiple opportunities to observe the mentor and other outstanding teachers. Opportunities for team-teaching or other forms of collaboration between the mentor and the mentee (and the new teacher and outstanding teachers) are also highly effective.

Optimal new teacher induction is *consistent and ongoing* and lasts a minimum of two years. Many induction programs start with great fanfare and diminish as the reality of day-to-day teaching as school activities take hold. Sadly, the time of year of highest anxiety and the need for new teachers does not occur at the beginning of the year.

Typically, new teachers come in excited, highly motivated, and happy. This honeymoon period usually lasts two to six weeks. By the beginning of October, things get a little harder and continue to get tougher until mid-November. Around Thanksgiving and the coming holiday season, most new teachers are relieved to finish their first semester. The time of greatest stress, anxiety, and difficulty for the average first-year teacher is the month of February.

It is a long time to June, the middle of winter, and a difficult time for students, teachers, and administrators. Unfortunately, it is also a time when little attention is paid to new teacher induction. It cannot be emphasized strongly enough that effective induction requires consistent application. Programs that diminish as the year progresses provide little benefit in terms of retention or improvement. Effective programs must be responsive during the most difficult times for new teachers.

CONCLUSION

New teacher induction that retains promising teachers and improves their teaching requires a healthy collegial and supportive school culture and a well-planned and implemented induction program. The most important element of an effective induction program is quality mentoring. As stated earlier, mentors need to be carefully selected, trained, and placed with new teachers. They should be compensated and provided release time to provide mentoring. Again, mentoring is extremely expensive, especially in time commitments.

Nonetheless, there is evidence (Dangel, 2006) that effective mentoring does have a large impact on new teacher retention and classroom performance. Mentoring also helps build a strong, instructionally oriented collegial culture in a school. For a final illustration, imagine a high school with one hundred faculty members with a high 20 percent annual turnover in faculty.

The school hires twenty new teachers and makes a huge investment of resources into mentoring and other induction services. This is an initial investment that, if the resources are used wisely, will have monetary benefits in the future.

For example, if the heavy expenditure of resources results in a reduction of the turnover rate to 10 percent annually, there will be ten less new teachers needing induction the following year. In addition, it will be ten less instructional personnel to recruit and hire, which is also an expensive processes. Consequently, the school will have a much higher return on investments in professional development and a range of additional costs associated with the hiring and development of teachers. Thus, it is money and time well spent! In closing, *if a school is able to identify, recruit, select, hire, and induct high-quality instructional personnel, they will have to spend much less time and money in the future identifying, recruiting, selecting, hiring, and inducting new personnel.*

Section III

DEVELOPING TEACHER QUALITY

Chapter 7

The Role of Assessing Teaching and Learning in Promoting Organizational Change

INTRODUCTION

The next three chapters focus on the continual professional growth of all teachers. Current research (Blankstein, 2013; Fullan & Quinn, 2016) provides consistent evidence that effective schools exhibit communities (teams) of professionals continually working together to improve the performance of each individual and the school as a whole. Success of functional professional learning communities requires two elements: individual teachers and communities of teachers must know what to change and how to change. The key to both elements is the relationship between teaching assessment and professional growth. Currently, school administrators devote a tremendous amount of time and energy observing and evaluating teachers. The purpose of these chapters is to examine how to get the most benefit, improved instruction, from teacher assessment. Stop to consider for a moment: Why do we evaluate teachers? Many successful teachers teach for many years and they are observed many times and evaluated annually.

At each evaluation, the principal shows the teacher the proper forms, asks the teacher to read them, and then asks the teacher to sign it. The ratings are typically high (Tucker, 1997); yet there are often a couple of comments like: "Mr. Johnson may want to consider additional methods of differentiating instruction as his students have multiple learning styles." The teacher is then given an electronic or paper copy of the evaluation, and in many cases, no one, including the teacher, ever reads the evaluations after they are completed and filed. Of course, if the teacher had not been doing his or her job, or had angered the principal in some way, the story might be different. Unfortunately, we know several distributing things about teacher evaluation:

1. Almost all schools conduct formal evaluations of teachers (Loup et al., 1996).
2. An extremely high percentage of teachers receive high scores across the board when rated using evaluation instruments (Tucker, 1997).
3. Most teachers believe that administrators use teacher evaluations as a form of coercion and control (Zepeda & Ponticell, 1998).
4. Individually, evaluations have a large impact on teacher efficacy, work satisfaction, and morale (Duke, 1990).
5. Teacher evaluations have the potential to have a large negative impact on the organizational culture of a school (Davis, Ellett, & Annunziata, 2002).
6. Data from formal observations of teaching are rarely used, or used appropriately, to improve the teaching and learning processes (Stiggins & Duke, 1988).
7. Most schools do not connect assessment of teaching and learning processes to professional development (Duke, 1990).

The essential point of this old, yet still relevant, research is schools generally do not effectively assess teaching for purposes of improving the teaching and learning process.

In a school, for the most part, teaching and learning is a *behavioral process* that occurs in a classroom between teacher and student interaction and student to student interaction. The teacher's role (job) is to ensure that the highest level of teaching (and as a result, learning) takes place in the classroom environment he or she is responsible for. In short, teaching is a *behavior*. As a result, any change (improvement) in teaching must include a change in the behavior of the teacher in the classroom. It is an egregious but nonetheless common error of leaders to underestimate the difficulty of affecting meaningful change in the behavior of professional adults—the phrase "herding cats" comes to mind.

The use of power, sanctions, and punishment is particularly ineffective in changing long-term behaviors of teachers. Strong group norms, high efficacy, and self-recognition of the benefits (personal, professional, moral) of behavioral change are particularly effective in changing long-term behavior. When professional teachers want to grow and progress, they must be provided with what they need to improve. This requires useful knowledge of the teaching and learning process occurring in each teacher's classroom. In the end, *shared instructional leadership* (Printy & Marks, 2003) does not exist in a school, unless there is intentional, systematic, and effective ongoing assessment of the teaching and learning process in every classroom and intentional, systematic, and effective utilization of the assessment data to improve the teaching and learning process. No single school administrator could begin to do any of this alone or with a small administrative team/staff. The assessment and development process described here requires the active participation of all professional practitioners in a school.

In thinking about this through an economic lens, there are two points to emphasize here. First, without a direct link to professional development, teacher assessment is inefficient (wasteful of time and money). Second, professional growth programs without a direct link to teacher assessment are inefficient and often ineffective. The next three chapters present and discuss the state-of-the-art teacher assessment and how it supports effective professional development.

This chapter focuses on Daniel Duke's (1990) enduring research that links professional development and assessment. The Case Reflection in this chapter is based on the author's research (Davis, Ellett, & Annunziata, 2002), which links leadership, organizational culture, and meaningful (affects changes in teaching behavior) teacher assessment practices.

PROFESSIONAL DEVELOPMENT VERSUS STAFF DEVELOPMENT

An ethos of professional development, grounded in assessment and improvement of the teaching and learning process, is a *cultural characteristic*. Assessment of practice and professional development support a culture of learning. Ethos is the disposition, character, or fundamental values peculiar to a specific group, culture, or movement. An ethos of assessment and development is characterized by the shared belief in the school that "we continually assess our teaching and learning in order to improve our teaching and learning."

This is consistent with the reasons to continually monitor and assess student learning during instruction. There are several things leaders can do to facilitate the development of a culture of learning. Perhaps the most important thing a leader can do to develop a culture of learning is to model ongoing personal assessment and development. This may include providing informal opportunities for feedback or more formal public assessments of his or her own job performance. The key is for the leader to be open to assessments of performance, encourage appropriate discourse about performance, and a willingness to change behavior.

This is consistent with what is asked of teachers. Leaders also need to model being well read, well informed, and professionally involved. In addition, it is critical that school leaders actively support professional discussion and collaboration. Professional discussion and collaboration are the key elements to positive change. The first part of this support is the assurance that professional discussion is safe. This requires professional relationships of trust. Ethical practice is the only way to provide such assurance, as unethical behavior on the part of an administrator destroys trust.

There are many ethical issues in administrative practice, but the most damaging (and common) ethical breaches of trust are the inappropriate use of administrative power. Zepeda and Ponticell (1997) found that over 70 percent of teachers surveyed believed principals used teacher evaluations as a means of intimidation and coercion. This is perhaps the most common abuse of power in the teacher evaluation process. It is especially damaging because when teachers perceive the evaluation process lacks integrity, the ability of the process to improve instruction is lost. The second thing leaders do to encourage discussion and collaboration is find ways to provide teachers with the time and resources they need to collaborate.

Duke (1990) argues professional growth (the terms "growth" and "development" are used interchangeably in this discussion of Duke—Duke uses the term "growth" but "development" is the generally accepted term used in practice) fosters uniqueness and virtuosity. That is, professional growth develops the unique talents of each individual teacher and promotes his or her reaching his or her full potential as a teacher.

Professional growth is not *remediation*. Remediation is a process for teachers who are not practicing at an acceptable level of performance (this is covered in chapter 10). Professional growth, on the other hand, is for teachers who have demonstrated proficiency in the basic standards of teaching. Duke labels these as *competent* teachers. Duke compares his view of "professional growth" with traditional types of what he calls "staff development" commonly provided in schools. Table 7.1 summarizes the key differences.

One key difference is between the goals of excellence and adequacy. A goal of *excellence* assumes that even the most proficient teacher can improve when professional learning is focused on areas of need. *Adequacy* goals are

Table 7.1 A Comparison of Professional Development and Staff Development in Schools

Professional Development (Growth)	*Staff Development*
Individual learning	Group learning
Cultivation of uniqueness and virtuosity	Collective growth in a common direction
Based on an individual's judgment of what is required to grow professionally	Guided by school and district goals
Requires teacher commitment, active participation (participatory learning)	Does not require teacher commitment and active involvement (sit-and-get)
Long term (connected process)	Short term (usually one session)
Excellence—realized full potential	Adequacy—minimum standards

group-oriented and designed to ensure all instructional personnel are able to meet minimum standards. Thus, a school might provide staff development on writing lesson plans to ensure all teachers know the minimum requirements for writing an acceptable lesson plan. There are two parts to professional growth related to assessment: capacity and opportunity. Both capacity and opportunity are based on social theorist Albert Bandura's (1997) notion of *efficacy*. For teachers, efficacy is an individual's belief that his or her practice will produce learning. It is a teacher's belief when he or she is teaching and the students are learning.

Capacity is a characteristic of the individual. Every competent teacher has a capacity for growth. Professional capacity equips teachers to "accomplish goals, undertake tasks, and overcome fears" (Duke, 1990, p. 132). *Opportunity* is a characteristic of the organization and a function of administrative leadership. There are three elements of increasing capacity and providing opportunity: motivation, awareness, and imagination.

For Duke, the primary tool a school leader has to *motivate* teachers is to provide opportunities to grow and acquire new skills. And while it is important to recognize that levels of motivation in individual humans do not remain constant, teacher who grow in practice have high expectations, are willing to risk, and view change and growth as positive. However, motivation is not enough, and teachers must be aware of how to improve practice. Duke lists five ways leaders may increase *awareness*:

- Breaking the normal professional routines of teachers.
- Changing the perspectives of teachers.
- Have teachers identify and examine assumptions.
- Expose teachers to professional literature.
- Provide performance feedback and the judgments of colleagues and supervisors.

Imagination includes the ability to redefine problems as opportunities and is encouraged through reflective practice. In addition, Duke highlights several school factors or characteristics of leaders who can influence an effective growth-oriented assessment processes. Leaders must have credibility as a source of performance feedback and be able to model the advice. A helping relationship of trust is required along with nonthreatening interpersonal manner. Patience and flexibility are the key. Suggestions for improvement need to be useful and based supported by a rationale for each suggestion. Duke also discusses policies that interfere with teachers' professional development. It is not helpful to punish teachers who fail to achieve ambitious goals while rewarding others who accomplish modest goals. It is also disruptive to convey expectations that all teachers should resemble each other in terms of professional skills and to treat professional growth as if it can be undertaken as part of teachers' normal duties. Time is essential: "If there is one consistent finding from research on teacher growth, it is that professional development takes time—time to interact with other educators, time to visit other schools and classrooms, and time to read and reflect" (p. 136). In other words, Duke states, consistent with all the HRD functions discussed in this text, assessment and professional development are expensive.

Like all other HRD processes, assessment for professional growth must be clearly planned in advance as part of *SHRP*. Here is a summary of Duke's five recommendations for designing growth-oriented evaluation (assessment) system:

1. Completely separate growth-oriented (formative) assessment of teaching and learning processes from accountability-based (summative) teacher evaluation systems.
2. Set aside time at the beginning of the professional development cycle to enhance teachers' awareness of growth possibilities.
3. Involve teachers in growth-oriented assessment: "Professional development is not something done to teachers. It is a process in which teachers must play an active role" (p. 137).
4. Prepare teachers and administrators for growth-oriented assessment through engaging in conversations on areas such as problem-solving, awareness-building, assumption-testing, and goal-setting.
5. Ensure that teachers feel safe to experiment and that the growth-oriented assessment is free from sanction.

CONCLUSION

All in all, the processes described in this chapter of assessing teaching and learning for purposes of professional growth represent a radical change in the typical evaluation and staff development activities in schools today. Nonetheless, it is the direction the field is moving in, as Professional Learning Communities (PLCs) continue to develop and grow. The problem is, of course, how do school leaders support the effective use of PLCs to improve instruction? Chapters 8 and 9 provide discussion and possibilities for consideration. Chapter 8 focuses on assessment of the teaching and learning process and chapter 9 addresses professional development; however, the topics will overlap and interconnect at many points.

Case Reflection 7

The Knight in Shining Armor

A study on a teacher assessment system identified vast differences between schools on the meaning, relevance, and effectiveness of the same teacher evaluation/assessment system. The study revealed that in-school leadership has an impact in their school on the overall opinions about teacher assessment, the knowledge of teacher assessment, the level of misinformation about teacher assessment, and the readiness of school personnel for implementing a new teacher assessment system. To illustrate the role that in-school leadership plays in teacher assessment, two leadership styles in two schools found in the interview results are compared and contrasted. These two examples represent extreme opposites of school-based leadership regarding teacher assessment. Two metaphors are used to describe these leadership styles: the first is labeled the *knight in shining armor* and the second *the talented musician in a small jazz combo*.

The principal described as the *knight in shining armor* was openly hostile toward formal teacher assessment. This principal believed that a new district teacher assessment system was a threat to teachers' professional careers and frequently expressed this concern to teachers. This placed the principal in the role of protecting the teachers from what he believed to be an uninformed, inconsistent, and hostile evaluation policy being unfairly forced on teachers by a heavy-handed central administration. During his interview, the principal said, "We have panic setting in. It is like a battlefield." The school leadership exhibited very low efficacy in regard to teachers' abilities to do well with the assessment system. The leader's attitude seemed to have permeated the interviewees at this school who described a climate of extreme fear of implementation of the new system. On the other hand, interviewees reported minimal or no site-based professional growth or training about the new system.

The culture of this principal's school, evident during the other interviews, was characterized by mistrust, fear, and misunderstanding of teacher assessment. Even teachers who tried to say positive things about the new system had little understanding of the goals and reasons for the change. The interviewees frequently expressed open hostility toward the new system and discussed how they were passively resisting the change. Interviewees who mentioned positive elements of the new system did not believe that it could ever work to effectively improve teaching and learning. Frequent concerns were expressed that the system was overwhelming, impossible to pass, and anti-teacher.

In contrast to the problems with the new assessment system in the school led by the *knight in shining armor*, the school fitting the description of the *leader of the small jazz combo* metaphor showed multiple indication of utilizing the new system for the improvement of teaching and learning and the benefit of students, teachers, and administrators. The *jazz combo* leadership metaphor describes a school in which the professional educators are working together toward the goal of quality teaching and learning. While there is a recognizable melody known by all (it could be the curriculum, school philosophy, or something of a teacher assessment system), all members of the organization are free to explore possibilities within the structures of the melody. The administrator of this type of organization uses his or her talents as an educator to facilitate subtle changes in the melody or move the melody to new levels; however, other members of the organization, primarily through their own skills, also have the ability to influence the music, or educational program, being delivered at the school. Everyone has a part in the leadership necessary to implement change in a way that might benefit the school.

The principal of the *jazz combo* school was enthusiastically supportive of the new assessment system. Monthly or bimonthly meetings were held with the school leadership to discuss the progress of the new system in the school. Interviews from the school indicated that the positive enthusiasm shown by the principal was found throughout the school. The interviews also indicated a climate of cooperation where professional personnel were functioning as a united team to ensure that the new system was integrated into their collective professional practice in a manner that improved teaching and learning. The value and potential of the new system was emphasized in the school through on-site staff development and training. The on-site training was structured so that the activities model the assessment indicators used in the system. The faculty was divided into small groups under the facilitation of assessment program leaders. The groups rotated so that during different meetings, individual faculty members always worked with a different assessment domain. For each domain, the groups went through the *Assessment Manual* and discussed the language and what it meant for their teaching and learning activities. Key words and critical thinking questions were provided to the groups and discussed to further assist the understanding and utilization of the domains in the classroom. All of the teachers interviewed at the school reported that they had high efficacy with regard to being successful with the new system. The concerns of the system discussed were much different than the *knight in shining armor* school because they were based on accurate information. Contrary to the emotionally laden fears described in the *knight in shining armor* school, the personnel at the *jazz combo* school discussed concerns with long-range planning, the lack of materials (manuals) available, time factors, and specific issues with individual domains. In addition, members of the Professional Growth Teams (collegial groups) at the school reported that they have met, planned, observed, and functioned as intended by the assessment processes. In short, the *jazz combo* school, evidently because of its leadership, was an exemplary model of successful teacher assessment for purposes of culture-building, professional growth, and improved teaching and learning.

Prompt

Individual school leaders have little direct control over district-wide teacher assessment practices, policies, and instruments. Most administrators use what they are provided with. As you know from the chapter, there is considerable variation nationwide in the quality of teacher evaluation. Nonetheless, the chapter argued that leadership is *the most important variable in the possibility of teacher assessment (evaluation) being a positive force (a culture builder and improver of teaching and learning) in the school organization*. Thus, administrators, through their leadership practice, have the ability to turn a *poor system into a positive* and the *best, state-of-the-art system* into a negative. Given this assumption, make as comprehensive a list as possible of administrator/leader "dos" and "don'ts" regarding teacher assessment.

Chapter 8

Methods and Value of Assessing Teaching and Learning Processes for Professional Growth

INTRODUCTION

As a whole, current processes for evaluating teachers are ineffective and inefficient. Sadly, just as the situation was beginning to improve nationwide at the turn of the century, the passage of the NCLB diverted attention to product as opposed to attention on process. Later, much of this focus on product was delegated to the states with the passage of Race to the Top (RTT) in 2009 (American Recovery and Reinvestment Act of 2009). Product is the measureable output obtained from educational services. The qualifying term measurable is important because the high-stakes accountability, which are dominant today, depend on measurement. Of course, in the case of current accountability models in most states, the primary measure is student achievement on common state or national-based performance assessments.

On the other hand, process refers to the act of production, which, in the case of education, is teaching and learning. Regardless, improving achievement (product/output) requires much more than analyzing and disaggregating output data to identify achievement gaps and areas of weakness. Placing the responsibility on teachers to improve without supporting the process of improvement is unlikely to result in a change in teaching behavior. Most teachers, especially poor-performing teachers, have limits in improving on their own. Thus, in order to produce sustained improvement in achievement, it is important to accurately assess the teaching and learning process in individual classrooms and for professional educators to work collaboratively to improve teaching and learning. Case Reflection 8 illustrates the problem with solely relying on standardized measures of student learning.

Case Reflection 8
A Football Analogy

Imagine that you are asked by your brother-in-law, who is a football coach in another state, to design a game plan to improve the offensive performance of his team during the next week (this is like an action plan for school improvement). To help you, he sends you some output data from the previous week's game (this is like disaggregated test scores):

Table 8.1 Game Statistics

First Downs Rushing	4
First Downs Passing	2
First Downs Penalty	2
Total First Downs	8
Rushes	30
Yards Rushing	75
Average Yards/Rush	2.5
Passing Attempts	21
Passing Completions	7
Completion Percentage	33%
Yards Passing	35
Average Yards/Comp.	5
Interceptions	2
Total Yards	110
Penalties	5
Yards Penalized	45
Fumbles/lost	2/1

Here is a game plan for the team based on the output data: bring the young men into the locker room and show them the stats and explain that they will be held accountable for future results. Then, remind them they must believe all players can score because the law says no player will be left behind. Explain if adequate progress is not made, the team may be taken over by the state and some of them may be replaced. Set arbitrary standards they need to obtain adequate per-game progress: for example in first downs (20), rushing yards (150), and completion percentage (50). Tell them to get out on the practice field and, unlike the previous game, they should try as hard as they can.

Prompts:

1. What role does quantitative output data play in identifying areas of need and providing the details needed to improve teaching and learning in classroom?

> 2. What are some of the limitations of using only student test scores to improve instruction?
> 3. How might both output and process data be combined to better support improved classroom teaching and learning?

While student achievement data are one indication of the quality of teaching and learning and is useful for identifying areas of strength and weaknesses, achievement data, nonetheless, provide no information on the details of the teaching and learning process. Yet the teaching and learning process produces the results measured by tests. This chapter provides an analysis and critique of current evaluation practices, a discussion of the *Personnel evaluation standards* (Gullickson, 2008), recommendations for developing and implementing a teacher evaluation system, and an overview of the state-of-the-art practices in teacher assessment. The purpose of this chapter is to promote the utility for assessing teaching and learning processes and to provide effective tools for leading assessment of teaching and learning to improve achievement. The focus is a structured and culture-oriented approach to developing an effective assessment process.

THE CURRENT STATE OF TEACHER EVALUATION

Teaching assessment and evaluation practices vary in multiple ways from state to state, district to district, and school to school. Variations include the quantity, quality, and purpose of teacher evaluation. Evaluation practices range from schools with few (or no) evaluations, perfunctory in quality, and used only as evidence in dismissal proceedings to schools that regularly conduct assessments of teaching and learning in a variety of ways to provide valuable data which is used to improve performance. Historically, there have been two large studies on teacher evaluation practices nationwide (Ellett & Garland, 1987; Loup et al., 1996). In the first study, Ellett and Garland (1987) found that typical practices are not effective.

While this research was over thirty years old, evaluation practices continue to have many of these same problems. The research found that teacher evaluation processes typically failed to reflect research on teaching, learning, and assessment. Most evaluation data were used for dismissal and remediation rather than professional development. There was a general lack of clear performance standards and teachers were rarely trained on the system used to evaluate them. In addition, most leaders who conduct evaluations were not trained to evaluate and poor inter-rater reliability was common.

External or peer evaluators were almost never used. There was also a lack of procedures to ensure reliability and credibility of evaluation data and processes. Ten years later, a follow-up study (Loup et al., 1996) found that policies at the local school district level still did not incorporate important teaching and learning elements identified in research. There was almost no change in the philosophical approaches to teacher evaluation. There was an increase in the use of evaluation for professional development but it was still not widespread. A general lack of training for teachers and evaluators remained. In addition, schools districts still did not take adequate measures to ensure the validity of their instruments and processes.

Since 1995, the major factor of change in teacher evaluation was NCLB (2002), RTT (2009), and the rise of statewide accountability models based on high-stakes testing. While there is no current research available on overall evaluation practices, it seems there has been little change. In fact, since the passage of NCLB and RTT, many sophisticated, research-based, and formative teacher evaluation systems have been canceled as districts have moved resources into test preparation (typically whole school reform programs or individual reading and numeracy programs) for RTT. This was the fate of the Professional Assessment and Comprehensive Evaluation System (PACES), an innovative and revolutionary system utilizing professional growth teams, developed in the Miami-Dade County School System by Chad Ellett in the late 1990s.

It was canceled in 2003 because of the "burden" it placed on teachers and administrators and other political pressures. A key hurdle in long-term implementation and support of transformative systems is that impactful evaluation systems are extremely political especially in large districts. In addition, if implemented in a meaningful manner, a new evaluation or assessment system, whether at an individual school, across an entire district, or all the public districts in a state, represents a significant change in the form of the professional practice teachers engage in. Because of the politics of change, it is difficult for leaders to prevent the dilution of comprehensive evaluation systems and to maintain them over time. From 1996 to 2003, the Miami-Dade County School System spent millions of dollars developing and implementing an evaluation system specifically designed to improve teaching and learning.

The system was designed internally and included full participation from the teachers' union; the United Teachers of Miami-Dade County (an affiliate of the AFT–PACES remains one of the only large-scale assessment systems to receive a full endorsement from a teachers' union). One of the many unique qualities of PACES was the extensive resources the district provided for training. The average amount of training on PACES across the district was two days for teachers and ten days for administrators. While the training was technically on PACES, in reality, it was a process-focused training designed to improve teaching and learning. In some schools, PACES was extremely successful.

The Jazz Combo school described in Davis, Ellett, and Annunziata (2002) remains an ideal model of what meaningful teacher assessment is able to accomplish. Unfortunately, the politics changed, the leadership in the district changed, and the system was scraped and replaced with a traditional check-and-file process. The field of education has a strong, research-based body of knowledge related to effective teacher evaluation to improve teaching and learning. Unfortunately, the knowledge of what works has failed to effectively influence policy and has had limited impact on practice.

In 1988, the Joint Committee on Personnel Evaluation Standards (joint committee) released the *Personnel evaluation standards* (standards). Although these standards were developed by a team representing fourteen leading national groups in education (AASA, AASPA, AERA, AEA, AFT, APA, AMECD, ASCD, ECS, NAESP, NASSP, ACME, NEA, NSBA), the standards were never widely adopted in the field. A second addition, *The personnel evaluation standards: How to assess systems for evaluating educators* (Gullickson, 2008) was published in 2008. The standards are an ideal resource available to a school leader interested in improving evaluation practices and utilizing evaluation practices to improve student achievement.

THE PERSONNEL EVALUATION STANDARDS (SECOND EDITION)

The standards are divided into four sections. The *propriety standards* are designed to ensure that personnel evaluations are legal, ethical, and conducted "with due regard for the welfare of the evaluatee and those involved in education." The *utility standards* are designed to ensure that evaluation is useful, timely, and informative. The *feasibility standards* are designed to ensure that evaluation practices are easy to implement, efficient, receive adequate funding, and are politically viable. The *accuracy standards* are designed to ensure that evaluations are technically valid and reliable and that they provide appropriate information to make correct decisions.

The purpose of the standards continues to be to improve the practice of educational personnel evaluation. Specifically, the work of the joint committee was focused on supporting the use of evaluation in the hiring process to "screen out unqualified persons from certification and selection."

Most importantly, effective evaluation practice "provides constructive feedback to individual educators" and "provides direction for staff development programs." It also allows school leaders fair systems to "recognize and reinforce outstanding service." Utilizing standards supports the use of evaluation data to "provide evidence that will withstand professional and judicial scrutiny" and to "provide evidence efficiently and at reasonable cost." Finally, the joint committee acknowledges the need to "aid institutions in terminating incompetent or unproductive personnel." In conclusion, the goal of the joint committee is for personnel evaluation to "unify, rather than divide, teachers and administrators in their collective efforts to educate students."

The joint committee based their work on the following *guiding assumptions*:

a. The purpose of personnel evaluation is to provide effective services to students and society.
b. Evaluation practices should be constructive and free from unnecessarily threatening or demoralizing characteristics.
c. Personnel evaluations are vital for planning sound professional development experiences.
d. Disagreements about what constitutes good teaching, good administration, and good research are warranted.
e. Personnel evaluations vary in complexity and importance.

The joint committee suggests teaching evaluation is useful for all of the key topics covered in this book: recruiting, hiring, induction, professional development, and termination. While standards provide a noteworthy template for thinking about evaluation practices, they lack specific details. Thus, this chapter concludes with important recommendations from Heneman and Milanowski (2003) on district-level teacher evaluation and then wraps up with an overview of the state-of-the-art in teacher evaluation and assessment at the building level.

RECOMMENDATIONS FROM HENEMAN AND MILANOWSKI

Heneman and Milanowski's (2003) report results of a mixed-methods research study that captures key issues that school administrators need to be aware of when assessing teachers and developing and implementing an assessment system. The recommendations, however, focus on design and implementation at the district level. The first useful recommendation is to *start with a competency model*. A competency model is a shared conception of effective teaching. Thus, the first step in designing a teacher assessment/ evaluation system is to clearly articulate a description of the components of effective teaching and learning.

The next step is to organize the description into a useable framework or model. It is critical that most teachers who will be assessed by the new system believe the model accurately describes and represents good teaching. Next, the district must *decide on the purpose* of the evaluation system. Heneman and Milanowski (2004) point out that summative evaluation system will cause considerable anxiety and stress for teachers. It needs to be recognized that this translates into damage of the organizational cultures of schools.

The authors do not make this point, but summative evaluation systems provide little benefit at a rather high cost (in other words, they tend to be inefficient). There are much more efficient means to deal with underperforming teachers (covered in chapter 10). Formative evaluation systems have considerable potential benefits (but the benefits depend on many factors) and may justify the high cost. Thus, formative evaluation systems can be efficient (have a high benefit-to-cost ratio).

The example of the knight in shining armor (Davis, Ellett & Annunziata, 2002) is a perfect example of the next recommendation to stress *implementation over instrumentation*. This research revealed vast differences among similar schools in the effective utilization of the PACES system. In one school, there was wholesale fear, distrust, and resistance. In the second school, there was a positive collegial culture utilizing PACES to rapidly improve student learning. In a nutshell, factors such as leadership, culture, and dispositions are more important than the evaluation instruments and policies.

As stated in the article, a good leader can make a poorly designed instrument effective and a poor leader can make a well-designed instrument ineffective. The fourth recommendation, *anticipate different and increased role expectation*, requires change in leadership practice. This is, perhaps, the biggest obstacle to meaningful assessment of teaching and learning. This change requires teachers, many who have practiced for many years, to radically change the way they engage in professional practice. The difficulty of this project should never be underestimated. The ability to promote a change in teacher behavior is the essence of leadership. Effective school leaders are individuals who have the knowledge and skills to radically change (improve) teaching and learning behaviors in classrooms.

If the teaching and learning behavior of teachers does not change in the classrooms, it is unlikely that improvement in output measures (achievement) will correlate with the long-term welfare of children! The next recommendation, *prepare teachers and administrators thoroughly*, is consistent with the previous emphasis on training. It is essential that teachers understand what they are being assessed on and how they are to use the assessment process to improve teaching and learning in the classroom. Administrators and other professionals conducting assessments must know how to recognize strengths and weaknesses during an observation.

Observations need to be consistent (reliable), accurate (valid), and beneficial. It is critical that assessors are able to communicate the results of their observations in a manner that allows teachers to learn and improve. One of the dominant themes of this book is the message that all HRD practices should be planned in advance (SHRP) and constitute one comprehensive HRD system.

Heneman and Milanowski's (2003) next recommendation concurs with the focus of this text and emphasizes this point: *align other HR management systems with the evaluation system*. Teacher evaluation and assessment systems fit especially well with teacher induction programs, mentoring, and professional growth. Finally, the Heneman and Milanowski (2003) recommend that districts should *evaluate the system*. It is difficult for any district, or expert in teacher evaluation, to develop and implement an evaluation system that does not have multiple problems.

The complexity of teaching and educational organizations, combined with the differences of individual community and district contexts, makes implementing any large-scale system a challenge. Like all management systems, an evaluation system will have elements that work well and elements that cause problems. Most of the problems will be associated with the specific context of each evaluation system. This is a good reason why districts and school should exercise caution when purchasing or implementing "canned" or prepackaged evaluation systems. Success of an evaluation system in one school is not an indication of the likelihood of success in other locations.

The research study of Davis et al. (2002) is an example of the type of evaluation that needs to be conducted in order to make improvements on a newly implemented evaluation system. Miami-Dade County piloted the PACES system for two years and conducted extensive quantitative and qualitative analysis before district-wide implementation. Building on these recommendations for design and implementation, this chapter concludes with some suggestions to address similar themes at the school building level.

OVERVIEW OF THE STATE-OF-THE-ART TEACHER ASSESSMENT AT THE BUILDING LEVEL

First, *take your time and involve all stakeholders in implementation*. At the school level, one of the worst mistakes that administrators make is to announce at the first faculty meeting that a new evaluation system is going to be used during the upcoming year. Regardless of the merits of a new system, a sudden introduction will introduce a high level of stress and uncertainty into the cultural dynamics of the school. Communication is the key to preparing teaching staff for change that will impact each one of them and this will take time. Ideally, the professionals in the school will have adequate time and opportunity to discuss the changes. It is especially important to allow teachers to ask questions.

The expression of concerns and criticisms of the change should be encouraged and addressed in a collegial and professional manner. It is not unprofessional for a teacher to disagree and resist a new evaluation system. Recalcitrant teachers can, and often do, win over once the culture of the organization changes. It is often counterproductive to use administrative power and authority to force a new system on a teaching faculty. In addition, *the teachers must believe that the assessment process recognizes and supports effective teaching and learning practices.* This requires a model that describes effective teaching (the school may have no control over this), and the observations and assessments must be fair, accurate, and consistent. It is a huge temptation for school administrators to utilize the teacher evaluation process to reward "team players" and punish "critics."

This is often an unconscious act on the part of the assessor because personal beliefs (likes and dislikes) influence what a person "sees" in a classroom (one reason why training is important). The goal for administrators is to assess every teacher on the same criteria and to be consistent with assessments over time (reliable). It is critical each individual rating accurately assesses the quality of teaching consistent with correct learning component identified. In other words, the evaluation instrument and measurement process must be valid (accurate) and reliable (consistent).

Like new systems at the district level, *the assessment process in the school should be subject to change and improvement.* Curriculum, standards, pedagogy, and other elements of professional teaching practice undergo continued change. More importantly, there will be problems and there will be opposing views in the school. Engaging stakeholders in the process of improving a teacher evaluation process will strengthen the culture.

People tend to be much more open to change in organizations where they believe their voice will be heard without retribution, and, if concerns are valid, appropriate modifications will be made. In linking evaluation to instruction, *classroom observations should focus on students.* Multiple teaching styles have been shown to be effective and observations that focus only on teacher behavior tend to have problems with validity and reliability. Learning occurs when students are engaged in the teaching and learning process and this is easily observable.

The logic of the observations should flow from unengaged students to a determination of why one, some, or all students are not engaged during any part of the lesson. If all students are engaged, the question becomes: What is the teacher doing that has all of the students fully engaged? In a similar manner, the process must *recognize, respect, and honor the complexity of teaching.* Currently, growing in popularity, many districts are advocating the "3 minute" walk-throughs as an effective supervisory practice. These walk-throughs may be effective and there is certainly much to be learned in three minutes; however, it is not a good practice for assessing teaching and learning for purposes of professional growth. The differences between a highly effective teacher and an average teacher are often subtle and not clearly evident on the surface. At a minimum, an entire lesson should be observed and assessed using a comprehensive model of effective teaching.

The purpose and focus of the entire process should be on professional growth. Teacher evaluation linked to professional growth is a planned and intentional process. Change and growth in student learning depend on changing professional behavior both in the administrative office and in the classroom. The only justification for the time and expense of assessing teaching and learning each classroom is professional growth. Professional growth is a process to produce change in teaching and learning in a classroom.

There needs to be flexibility in the system and process. *Be aware that evaluation systems and processes may not fit all types of teachers and classrooms the same or well and make modifications as needed.* There are some teachers and classrooms (special education, PE, art, music, drama, etc.) that are not easy to assess using traditional methods. The ability to assess these classrooms is enhanced when the focus of the assessment is on student engagement. While a teacher of a PE or a special education class might utilize a nontraditional method, it is still critical that students be engaged. All assessment should begin with student engagement and this is observable in all class settings, regardless of the subject.

It is also important to include teachers in the process by *involving master teachers in peer observation and collegial improvement efforts and allowing all teachers the opportunity to observe colleagues.* Effective observation and assessment of every classroom is simply too much for a small number of administrators to accomplish alone. The most effective method of changing teaching and learning behaviors in classrooms is through collegial effort resulting in shared professional norms within a school. Simply, behavior change is most likely when group norms change and this is a collegial process. The point of view changes from "something my principal is making me do" to "we work together to improve because that is what we as teachers in this school do."

Admittedly, this is much easier said than done as teachers are often highly resistant and uncomfortable with peer observation. But there are also examples (Davis, Ellett, & Annunziata, et al. [2002]) where peer observation works well. Likewise, *devote as much time as possible to teacher training.* Training provides information, examples, and opportunities to discuss and practice the procedures of the evaluation process. Training reduces anxiety and builds collegial and cultural support for changes. Training allows teachers to express concerns and make recommendations for improvement. Ultimately, training is the mechanism through which a teacher assessment processes becomes an effective tool for improving professional development. The entire effort depends on the teachers' understanding as to how to use the assessment process to improve their own practice.

CONCLUSION

The challenge for building-level administrators is that the implementation of the recommendations in this chapter is more expensive and difficult than any other HRD function presented in this book. Systematically linking assessment of teaching to professional growth, however, also has the most potential to transform teaching and learning in a school. While the cost is high, the reality is that the entire professional energy of an administrative and instructional staff should focus on assessing and improving the teaching and learning process. This seems like the most logical suggestion in the world; however, for a variety of reasons, most schools still do not accurately assess the actual teaching and learning process.

Schools dance around the topic with whole school reform models, new curriculum programs for literacy and numeracy, increased school days, increases in time devoted to math and language instruction, and never-ending test preparation. States, districts, and schools hold teachers and administrators accountable for results, and they threaten and provide various sanctions for failure. Policymakers develop pay-for-performance systems and other incentives designed to motivate teachers to perform higher quality work.

States develop and institute new curricula combined with new standards to be assessed by an ever-increasing array of tests. Some schools even implement systems where instruction is scripted down to the point of teachers being told exactly what they will say and do at any given moment in the lesson, including specific responses to "any" question a student might ask. States and institutions of higher learning devote extensive money to redesign teacher and principal preparation programs. Regardless of all this, the teaching profession still does a poor job of assessing the teaching and learning process to help teachers improve! And yet the field of education has ample research-based evidence supporting how to do this.

Yes, meaningful assessment is difficult and time-consuming and school-based leaders must operate with lack of resources (money and time) to implement this type of change. Lack of time and money are likely the primary reasons that assessment practices are not effectively utilized in many schools. There is often a lack of knowledge of how to link assessment to improve teaching and learning. Given this, consider this question: In your school, would you prefer a student to receive three hours a day of low-quality numeracy instruction or one hour a day of the highest quality numeracy instruction? Poor instruction is a waste of resources. This mandates that teachers and leaders should learn how to use assessment data to improve, take the time and effort to focus on improving, and choose a disposition to change which allows for new teaching practices to emerge.

Chapter 9

Leadership and Developing Human Resources in Educational Organizations through Professional Development

INTRODUCTION

The goals of the previous two chapters were to develop knowledge and skills in improving HRD planning for teacher evaluation and professional growth. The emphasis now shifts to connecting the assessment of teaching and learning to professional growth. This chapter continues the focus on the role of leadership in improving student achievement. The goal is to provide educational leaders with practical ideas and tools to implement in professional practice through the assessment of the teaching and learning processes.

THE ROLE OF PROFESSIONAL GROWTH IN HRD

The foundation of professional growth is adult learning. Not surprisingly, adults learn in a similar manner as children learn. In other words, effective pedagogical practices for children are also effective pedagogical practices for adults. Differences are based on age-related levels of cognitive development. Specifically, young children are much more receptive and cognitively able to acquire new knowledge and develop new cognitive networks. The implication of this for professional development is adults do not learn well in passive learning environments.

On the contrary, adults learn best when they have control of their own learning, value and have the desire to learn the material, and are actively involved in critical thinking and problem-solving (Arghode, Brienger, & McLean, 2017; Malik, 2016). In this chapter, staff development is used to reflect traditional practices of using programs selected by authorities in power (principals) and delivered by experts with presentations to large groups of passive teachers in isolated subjects, and topics result in little learning (content is typically a review of what teachers already know) and even less change in teaching behavior in the classroom.

To make a difference, professional development involves teachers and other stakeholders with planning and delivering development processes and practices that are continual, relevant, based on assessed needs and school goals, and actively engages the participation of recipients. This chapter provides a framework for planning this type of professional development. While the framework is presented in the context of planning, it also provides a nice overview of best practices in professional development.

A FRAMEWORK FOR PROFESSIONAL DEVELOPMENT LEADERSHIP

First, the effective professional development in a school is a well-thought-out, intentional process. Proper planning is essential. Recall the most important element of the SHRP process described in chapter 3 and the purpose of SHRP to connect all HRD activities together in one integrated whole, focusing on student achievement. Growth depends on changing professional behavior both in the administrative office and in the classroom. Professional growth is the systemic process through which sustainable change in teaching and learning behavior takes place in the classroom. Table 9.1 provides a guide for planning a professional development program.

Table 9.1 Planning a Professional Development Program

Activity	Explanation
Review of Existing Practices	The first step is to assess the existing professional development process
Analysis of Output Data	The next step is the analysis of disaggregated achievement data (gap analysis)
Determine Specific Goals	Results of the gap analysis are used to determine specific target achievement goals
Assessment of Teaching and Learning Processes	A process is developed to link assessment of teaching and learning, performance goals, and professional development
Activities	Professional development activities are planned and coordinated
Estimating Costs	Monetary and time costs of the plan are estimated to ensure that the plan is appropriate and feasible, given the resources available

(Continued)

Table 9.1 (Continued)

Activity	Explanation
Evaluation	A process for evaluating the effectiveness, strengths, and weaknesses of the professional development program is prepared in advance
Modifications/New Planning	Results of the evaluation are used to make modifications in the professional development program during the next cycle of SHRP

The emphasis here is that planning for professional growth, as well as SHRP in general, is not a discrete or isolated process. Planning for professional growth needs to fit with other areas of SHRP, including hiring, induction, and assessment of teaching and learning, and this needs to fit all other organizational planning. The ties that bind all planning together are the mission, vision, and goals of the organization. While strategic objectives do vary, this overview will assume an objective of improved student achievement for the purpose of discussing the activities presented in table 9.1. Again, while details are not included (these should be worked out in specific contexts), it is critical that the planning process involves stakeholder collaboration. Teachers are essential for planning effective professional growth.

The process begins with a *review of existing practices*. An old farmer once said, "If it ain't broke, don't fix it." Often times in education, especially with a change in administration or new mandates for reform, educational leaders rush in and create change with new programs or initiatives without assessing what has been working or not working in current systems. Even worse, it is common for new programs to be initiated with great fanfare and expense only to be abandoned two or three years later, without any formal assessment of success or failure. Thus, the first step in planning a professional development program is to assess current professional development activities and processes. While this is not likely to be in the form of a formal program evaluation, there should be a discussion of the following questions and topics:

- Who planned the current process and how?
- What activities are included in the current process?
- How much time and money is available for the current process?
- How were topics/presentations selected for the current process?
- How are teachers actively involved in the current process?
- How do current processes fit with the goals of the school?
- How do current processes reflect the use of data?
- How do current processes reflect assessment of the teaching and learning process?

- In what ways does the current system meet, or fail to meet, the professional growth necessary to accomplish the goals of the school?

Depending on the answers to these and other questions, planning for professional development may only require minor adjustments of current practices or it may require the complete replacement of existing practices with a new process.

Effective professional development is data-based. Following review and assessment of existing development activities, an *analysis of output data* is warranted. There are two kinds of data used to drive professional development: quantitative (primarily output) and qualitative (primarily process). In the case of professional development, process data, or assessment of teaching and learning, is part of the implementation of professional development. Output data, however, are used to identify specific content areas of focus during planning.

There are multiple types of quantitative data that may be used in planning professional development. While there are many processes available for analyzing and using data, gap analyses are particularly useful because they are simple and effective. A gap analysis uses discrete (disaggregated) measures of dependent variables (effects—may be student achievement or a correlate of student achievement such as attendance or discipline referrals) to compare current performance to desired performance. Table 9.2 provides a list of

Table 9.2 Commonly Available Data Types Used in Schools and Options for Disaggregation

Data Source	Types	Subgroups for Disaggregation
Achievement Test Data	State, national, NAEP, norm-referenced, criterion-referenced	Race/ethnicity, gender, subject, grade level, SES, English as Second Language student (ESL), special education, teacher
Enrollment	Honors/AP classes, college track, special education	Race/ethnicity, gender, SES
Dropout Rate	Transfers, expulsions, attendance, not in school	Race/ethnicity, gender, SES
Discipline Referrals	Fighting, disrespect to teacher, class disruption	Teacher, race/ethnicity, gender, SES
Attendance	Absences, tardies, in-school suspension, out-school suspension	Race/ethnicity, gender, SES
Graduation Rates	Overall, on time, GED, certificate	Race/ethnicity, gender, SES, special education, ESL
Grades	GPA, class rank, core course repeats	Race/ethnicity, gender, SES, subject, teacher
Retention Rates	Grade level, summer school participation, course repeats	Race/ethnicity, gender, SES, subject, teacher
Special Education	All types	Race/ethnicity, gender, SES

commonly available data sets and areas of disaggregation. The gap analyses will provide the data needed to *determine specific goals*.

Based on the objectives in the strategic plan and state/federal performance standards, a specific set of outcome goals will guide the professional development program. The key guideline for determining outcome goals is that they be realistic and obtainable. It is important to realize that serious problems may be revealed in the data and deeply entrenched systemic, cultural, or contextual problems may not be solvable in one or two years. The important thing is to make steady progress and improvement. Table 9.3 provides an example of a gap analysis and goal determination for each of the nine types of data listed earlier for a hypothetical middle/high school in rural North Mississippi:

Table 9.3   Data Examples for Gap Analyses and Goal Determination

No.	Actual Data	Target	Gap	One Year Goal
1	49% of black students scored at or above the proficient level on the eighth grade reading portion of the state assessment compared to 91% of white students	95%	46%	65% of black eighth grade students will score at the proficient level
2	38% of students enrolled in AP classes are boys	50%	12%	44% of students enrolled in AP classes will be boys
3	Forty-two Hispanic males dropped out of school past year	0	42	Less than twenty Hispanic males will dropout next year
4	82% (261) discipline referrals were from 10% (eight) of the teachers in the school	<100 referrals	161	The eight teachers will reduce discipline referrals by 75%
5	Average daily attendance was 91.5%	95%	3.5%	Average daily attendance will improve to 93%
6	26% of economically disadvantaged students graduate in four years	80%	54%	35% of economically disadvantaged students will graduate in four years
7	62% of all ninth graders are failing Algebra the first time	<10%	52%	Less than 25% of all ninth graders will repeat Algebra
8	45% of all eighth grade students must take summer school to advance to the ninth Grade	<10%	35%	Less than 20% of all eighth grade students will have to go to summer school to advance to the ninth grade
9	Black students are 5.2 times more likely to be receiving special education services than any other racial/ethnic group	N/A	N/A	N/A

A couple of points about these examples: first, in most cases, the goals will focus on achievement data; however, many of the examples provided are strong correlates to achievement. Second, there is a varying degree in the role professional development may play in obtaining these goals. Nonetheless, professional development potentially plays a key role in improving in all of these areas. All of the types of data presented (except perhaps # 9) are impacted by what happens in the classroom.

In addition to existing output data, there is also a need to *assess the teaching and learning processes*. The goals by themselves are not enough. Although goals identify specific problems to be focused on, they do not answer the questions of why a problem in the classroom exists and how it is best addressed. For example from the table 9.3, why are black students scoring at the proficient level on the eighth grade state reading assessment at a rate 42 percent less than white students? What is happening in the classroom and what might be changed in the classrooms to decrease this gap? Or, what happened in the classrooms of the eight teachers in example 4 to result in 214 referrals past year?

The need during the planning process for professional development is to develop a plan to focus on teachers, classrooms, and teaching and learning processes related to the established goals. Specifically, what is going to be assessed, how are the assessments going to take place, and how is the assessment data going to be used (linked to professional development)? Of course, a meaningful process for assessing teaching and learning should already be in place.

This will allow this part of the process to determine how the existing assessment system will be used to provide data-based guidance for professional development. The assessment of teaching and learning in the classroom then provides the data needed to plan *professional development activities*. This part of the process develops and clearly articulates a plan for how administrators and teachers will work together in teams to improve teaching and learning, or address other identified issues, to obtain the target goals. It is important here to keep in mind the principles of adult learning presented earlier in the chapter emphasizing adults learn best when they actively participate in their own learning.

Once the plans are in place, the next step is to ensure teachers and have the organizational support needed to be successful. A vital part of planning for professional development is to create a feasible program; therefore, it is critical to ensure that the resources, both material and time, are available by *estimating costs* of the planned professional development program. It is a waste of effort to plan a process requiring time and money not available. Thus, it is necessary for planners to estimate with a high degree of accuracy exactly what is going to be asked of administrators and teachers in terms of time and effort, and how much the plan is going to cost.

CONCLUSION

Whatever professional development plan is developed, its success will depend on teacher buy-in. This is where leadership (from both administrators and teachers) comes in. There is nonetheless the need to be certain that the resources are available to accomplish what is being asked. Whatever plan and process is developed, it is not a finished product. Effective professional development is an ideal process to model continuous improvement; therefore, to support this process is critical to plan for meaningful *evaluation* of the professional development program. Evaluation is a continual process of planning, engaging in the process, evaluating the process, and making modifications/improvements and planning for the next year. At the time of initial planning, it is important to determine how you will evaluate the program as it is being implemented.

How will successful implementation of the program be defined and what type of data will be collected along the way to be used in the evaluation process? This is a formative evaluation process and the goal is ongoing improvement in the professional development in the school. What is working? What is not working? What might be improved and what needs to be eliminated? Once a cycle (typically a year) has been completed, the final step is *modifications and new planning*. At the initial planning stage, there is little to do in this area. The important thing to be aware, however, is the entire process will take place again at the end of the cycle. Hopefully, if the current process is well done, the process next year will be much easier and less time-consuming. In conclusion, effective professional development requires effective planning integrated with other teaching and learning processes and operational management.

Case Reflection 9

Review of the Link between Assessed Needs, Organizational Goals, and Professional Development Processes

Conduct a review on a school's professional development program based on the previous three chapters. Provide a short description related to each of the following prompts and some suggestions for positive changes that could be made:

Prompts:

1. Does professional development in the school focus on individual learning or group learning?
2. Is professional development in the school based on clearly identified goals based on clearly defined needs?
3. Is professional development in the school based on individual's judgment of what is required to grow professionally or by school and district goals?
4. Does professional development in the school require individual commitment or active participation?
5. Is professional development in the school a short-term or a long-term effort to target specific improvements?
6. Does the goal of professional development in the school strive for excellence and realized full potential or adequacy and minimum standards?

Section IV

MISCELLANEOUS

Chapter 10

Dealing with Marginal Teachers

THE PROBLEM OF INCOMPETENT TEACHERS

The purpose of this chapter is to address the issue of incompetent teaching and provide some suggestions for dealing with incompetent teachers. The foundation for understanding issues in dealing with marginal teachers is founded on the work of Pamela Tucker (1997). Teachers provide the core of teaching and learning in schools. Simply, how well teachers perform in their job determines the level of student learning. Tucker acknowledges that most teachers perform their jobs with a high level of commitment to their professional duties; however, she also notes "that a small minority of teachers do not, or are unable, to perform their professional duties at an acceptable level" (p. 104). While most professional educators have an experience-based understanding of unacceptable teaching, Tucker's research required a precise definition of teacher incompetence. Typically, teacher incompetence refers to "failure to perform at an acceptable level" (p. 104); however, Tucker emphasizes it is also an important term with a precise definition describing grounds for dismissal of teachers in thirty-one states (1997, p. 105).

The actual level of incompetent teachers in schools is a matter of debate and difficult to measure for a variety of reasons. There are many reasons to believe, however, the number is at an unacceptable level. In general, levels of performance in many schools and in many classrooms are well below the societal expectations. Certainly, there are many causes for this and classroom teachers should not be singled out for blame. On the other hand, it is hard to find a parent or an educational professional without a story and example of poor teaching. While there is no accurate data on the number of teachers formally and informally dismissed from the profession nationwide, we do know there is evidence (Tucker, 1997) the number is relatively small and many incompetent teachers remain in the classroom year after year. One of the reasons there are poor data on teacher dismissal is the frequency of informal methods used to remove teachers.

Often, teachers are either counseled out (asked to resign in lieu of dismissal, or the bad evaluation if you stay and good evaluation if you leave ploy), transferred, or forced out by poor treatment (bad classrooms, the worst students, ostracism). While these practices are common, they are also unprofessional, unethical, and detrimental to a positive school culture. Tucker cites two studies on the number of teachers removed for incompetence. In the first, Educational Research Service (1988) found a 0.5 percent termination rate for tenured teachers over a two-year period. Given this includes both induced resignations and dismissal, and a two-year time period, these data found that, in 909 school systems, only one in 400 teachers were removed each year for incompetence in the classroom. The number actually dismissed is likely much less.

In the second study, Bridges (1992) found an annual dismissal rate of 0.6 percent (1 in 167); however, only 5.2 percent of these (1 in 2,976) were tenured teachers. Tucker's study (1997, p. 108) found the percentage of tenured teachers recommended for dismissal in one year to be 0.1 percent (1 in 1,000). Tucker builds her research on existing factors that inhibit administrative action to incompetence that outweigh the factors that facilitate response. In other words, from our economic perspective, the costs of dismissing incompetent teachers, especially tenured teachers, is considered to be greater than the benefits.

Tucker (1997) identified many reasons why administrators decide not to take action to dismiss incompetent teachers. First and likely the most common today is fear of the time and cost of *potential litigation*. Even if there is no legal challenge to a termination, the process involves *excessive expenses*, especially when the time involved is recognized as a cost. In addition, the termination of a teacher needs to be based on valid data and *ambiguity about the teacher evaluation criteria* in a dismissal process will likely end in failure.

On a more personal note, as human beings, school leaders tend to experience *discomfort with conflict*, the *negative effect on school climate*, and the polarization of faculty that the termination of a teacher will often cause. Further, dismissing a teacher results in *role conflict for principal* who needs to be viewed as a supporter and advocate to facilitate continuous cycles of improvement. Along with the role conflict, in termination situation there may often be a *sense of isolation for the principal*.

Given these problems, Tucker's study sought to identify administrative and contextual factors supporting successful removal of incompetent teachers.

Tucker found the following components of an evaluation system support effectively dealing with marginal teachers:

a. clear performance criteria,
b. general evaluation procedures,
c. remedial procedures,
d. organizational commitment to evaluation,
e. level of teacher-administrator collaboration,
f. evaluator training, and
g. integration of evaluation in the other functions of the organization.

Tucker's findings on inhibiting factors on administrators in seeking dismissal of incompetent teachers were similar to existing literature with some notable exceptions. Tucker found that personal characteristics impacted an administrator's motivation to confront problem teaching.

The most common example is discomfort with conflict. Interestingly, and new to the literature, Tucker found that many administrators lack the skills and training to successfully dismiss incompetent teachers (1997, p. 116). In addition, Tucker found that many principals cited lack of support from superintendents and boards in removing incompetent teachers from the classroom. Finally, Tucker found that a lack of financial resources (including the cost of litigation) discouraged action.

Given these results, Tucker makes some key recommendations for successful dismissal of incompetent teachers. First, there must be a unified political will among principals, superintendents, and school boards to remove incompetent teachers. Second, there needs to be a sustained organizational commitment of resources. Finally, principals need effective training on summative evaluation and dismissal processes and procedures.

The next section provides a summary overview of some key issues in dismissing incompetent teachers. First, removing incompetent teachers from the classroom may well be the most difficult thing a school administrator does. Incompetent teachers tend to be good people in the wrong role. They are human beings with careers, families, hopes and dreams, and friends and supporters within the school and the community. Sadly, dismissal of a teacher is usually harmful to his or her career, finances, self-esteem, and overall well-being. In addition, the process almost always has a negative impact on other individuals in the organization and the overall culture of the school. If handled appropriately and there is due process and a recognition of justice (stakeholders perceive the dismissal decision and process to be fair), the negative effects tend to be limited and short in duration.

The decision to implement a dismissal process involves one the most sensitive ethical dilemmas in the profession. In its simple form, the dilemma is between the well-being of an incompetent teacher and the educational needs of the students. The hard part of the dilemma stems from the difficulty in adequately measuring the effect (or lack of effect) of an individual teacher and from determining when to transfer the HR goal from remediation to dismissal.

In regard to the organizational culture, teachers in a school usually know who the incompetent teachers are. In addition, most effective teachers prefer an increase in the overall level of practice in the profession and desire the removal of ineffective teachers. On the other hand, teachers also tend to be highly sensitive to displays of the administrative authority necessary to remove a teacher. By its very nature, the process tends to incubate an us-versus-them mentality between professional teachers and school administrators. Further, it is common for teachers to like and care about the teacher being dismissed. This is one reason why informal methods may cause more harm than good. If administrators put informal pressure on a teacher and the teacher fails to resign, the initiation of dismissal proceedings often takes on the appearance of a "witch hunt."

Given these issues, the decision to dismiss a teacher from employment must be made only when there is a strong consensus among the leadership team supported by classroom assessment and performance that teaching and learning in the teacher's classroom is at an unacceptable level and improvement is not likely to occur. Even then, the dismissal process must provide a genuine opportunity for the teacher to improve and remain in the classroom. Following is a discussion of things to consider before and after the decision has been made to initiate a dismissal process against a teacher. Most districts have specific dismissal policies with common elements but differ in specific procedures and details.

Regardless, it is important to pay attention to the *HR practices that support successful dismissal of incompetent teachers*. The foundation for success is a valid data document that the teacher is not abiding by the teaching and learning expectations defined in the contract. The data must be based on the *use of a valid teacher evaluation system*. The evaluation instrument must stand up in court as an accurate measure of effective and ineffective teaching. Observation and evaluation data for all teachers should have high levels of variability and inner and inter-rater reliability. If one observer rates a teacher high and another observer rates the teacher low or if an administrator rates a teacher high on several evaluations and then suddenly starts recording low ratings, the data do not hold up well under scrutiny.

Variability is achieved by avoiding "perfect" observation and evaluation reports for "all" teachers. Simply, a process that rates most teachers with all perfect scores is not credible. In addition, *evaluation procedures must be followed*. It is necessary to show that all teachers have been observed and evaluated the same way under the procedural guidelines of the evaluation systems. Many cases are dismissed because the defendant was able to show that evaluation policies were not followed consistently by the administration resulting in the process being deemed arbitrary and capricious by the court.

Procedures for dismissing teachers for incompetent teaching need to be *separated from other disciplinary actions* (absences, tardies, professional behavior, abuse, insubordination, etc.). It is common for teachers with instructional problems to also have other behavioral issues. Regardless, the argument needs to focus on the teacher's inability to instill learning in children. This is the case the administrator needs to develop and support with evidence. A strong case is supported by a leader who *maintains accurate records of all observations and evaluations, and document all meetings and communications*.

In addition to the procedural details, principals must *know and be fully trained on personnel law and district policies and procedures*. As a leader the principal needs the organizational vision, will, moral purpose, and commitment to remove incompetent teachers from the classroom. This commitment includes planning for the time and a reserve of resources to support dismissal proceedings. An authentic professional learning community characterized by professional behavior, collegial practice, and shared commitment to continuous improvement where outstanding teaching is the norm is not tolerant of poor teaching. With this level of culture, the dismissal process symbolically becomes an unfortunate but necessary enforcement of group norms rather than an act of authority by an administrator with power against a teacher with less power. A leader should have a policy and procedure for determining when, based on evaluation data, dismissal proceedings will be initiated.

There are several things to consider once a decision to initiate dismissal proceedings has been made. Dismissal decisions should always be made in collaboration with the superintendent or central office and it is essential that the building-level administrator has full support from the district. Rules and procedures vary among districts and it is necessary to always review district policies and procedures for dismissal of teachers, especially procedures to maintain the rights and confidentiality of the marginal teacher. Collect and review all supporting documents for accuracy, consistency, and compliance with policies and procedures. A final review of the decision is to initiate dismissal proceedings is warranted focusing on evidence that the teacher is unlikely to positively respond to additional remediation efforts.

AN EXAMPLE OF DISMISSAL PROCEEDINGS (DUE PROCESS)

This example is provided as a guide with the understanding that the employment laws differ from state to state, personnel policies differ from district to district, and each school and community context is different. This example is provided to present typical procedures followed in successful termination proceedings:

1. Notify the teacher in writing that, based on assessed teaching performance, dismissal proceedings are being initiated. Include a detailed description of the process, timeline, and full disclosure of the teacher's legal rights. Be clear that an opportunity and support will be provided for improvement.
2. Provide an opportunity for a meeting or hearing to discuss documented performance, expected performance, and provide details of the assistance plan. Teachers should have access to performance data prior to the meeting and an opportunity to rebut the data in front of an impartial tribunal. The teacher has a right to counsel during this hearing.
3. Upon recommendation from the tribunal, the teacher is placed in an assistance program designed with the goal of improving performance to an acceptable level. It is essential that the program include frequent assessment and feedback to the teacher. The assistance program should last a minimum of 120 school days. At this stage of the process, it is critical that the goal for everyone involved needs to be addressing the pedagogical issues and retaining the teacher. Remediation is *not* a process to be checked off prior to implementation of a decision already made!
4. A reevaluation based on observations and student data of the teacher's performance is conducted during and at the end of the assistance program. If the teacher is assessed as acceptable, the teacher begins a two-year probationary period with three evaluations per year. During the probation period, an "unacceptable" overall rating on any evaluation will result in a return to the assistance program.
5. Failure of and the "End-of-Assistance-Plan Assessment" will result in the scheduling of a termination hearing before the tribunal. The teacher is allowed counsel and the opportunity to call witnesses and to provide evidence in support of his or her teaching.
6. The tribunal can vote to dismiss or for another 120 school days in the assistance program.
7. The teacher has the right of appeal against the tribunal's decision to a subcommittee of the school board.

CONCLUSION

Again, the specific form and details of this process vary considerably among districts and even within districts (union districts tend to have much more detailed processes and provide the teachers with more opportunities for improvement and review). Procedures also vary based on the tenure status of the teacher. Regardless, any dismissal process is difficult, time-consuming, and expensive. At this point, the key question is, is it worth it? Wright, Horn, and Sanders (1997) provide a strong answer based on their research on the Tennessee Value-Added Assessment System:

> Despite ongoing debates about whether, and how much teachers make a difference in student learning relative to a host of other factors assumedly affecting student learning, and whether particular elements of teaching can be systematically and causally linked to student achievement, the results of this study well document that the most important factor affecting student learning is the teacher. In addition, the results show wide variation in effectiveness among teachers. The immediate and clear implication of this finding is that seemingly more can be done to improve education by improving the effectiveness of teachers than by any other single factor. *Effective teachers appear to be effective with students of all achievement levels, regardless of the level of heterogeneity in their classrooms.* If the teacher is ineffective, students under that teacher's tutelage will achieve inadequate progress academically, regardless of how similar or different they are regarding their academic achievement. . . . Thus, classrooms of very effective teachers, following relatively ineffective teachers make excellent gains but not enough to offset pervious evidence of less than expected gains. (pp. 63–64)

What this famous research says is bad teachers harm kids academically in ways that are lasting and almost impossible to remediate.

Case Reflection 10
The Mad Coach

Introduction:

You are the principal of a large urban middle school with a wide range of extracurricular activities and severe limitations of space before, during, and after school. The issues of space have been compounded by the behavior of one of the PE teachers, Ms. Shiny Earlyriser. Over the past several years, you have been increasingly dissatisfied with Ms. Earlyriser's teaching. You have encouraged Ms. Earlyriser to adapt current changes in physical education and incorporate a wide range of educational activities related to health and fitness. You also expect Ms. Earlyriser, like you do all teachers, to include instruction in language arts and mathematics in her curriculum. In addition, you want to see regular physical activities and the students in her class developing skills of teamwork and cooperation in active sporting activities. In support of this effort, you have provided Ms. Earlyriser multiple curriculum materials, sports equipment, and sent her to a professional development conference. Regardless, during four checks during the past month, you observed Ms. Earlyriser's students playing disorganized no-rule volleyball without supervision, while a majority of students sat on the bleachers socializing and horsing around.

Unrelated to her teaching, Ms. Earlyriser has also been a problem in her role as girls' basketball coach. Her team has only won four games in the last two seasons, the team only has twelve players, and parents are frequently complaining. Ms. Earlyriser also has repeatedly made an issue out of the gym schedule. Several years ago, based on a request from parents who wanted their daughters to have free time in the afternoon to pursue other activities, the leadership team led a process involving stakeholders to develop a schedule to meet the desires of the parents. While the schedule did include a very early start, additional time was provided to the young women on the basketball team with a first hour PE course. Nonetheless, Ms. Earlyriser has continued to make an issue out of the schedule even though you have offered to revisit the issue with the leadership team and a new gym, currently under construction, will be available next year. If parents are willing to support an afternoon practice, space will be available. Currently, the gym schedule is as follows:

5:00 a.m.—7:30 a.m. (8:40 end with PE) Girls Basketball
3:00 p.m.—6:00 p.m. (2:00 start with PE) Boys Basketball
6:30 p.m.—9:00 p.m. Wrestling

Situation:

Early in the week, you notified Ms. Earlyriser that her performance was unacceptable and that you are placing her on an improvement plan. You informed her in writing that the goal is to retain her as teacher and that she will be provided full support in improving her performance, including a reduced schedule and extensive professional development. You also informed her that the process is the first step in formal dismissal proceedings and a failure to improve and meet clearly stated expectations would result in a continuation of the next phase of the dismissal process. She has been advised of her due process rights and rights to counsel.

Today, you received the following e-mail from Ms. Earlyriser:

Mr. Goodoldboy,

I have had enough of the unfair treatment by your administration of the young women on the girls' basketball team. For the past five years you have promised to make changes in the gym schedule; and yet, nothing has changed. Even if the new gym is completed on time, it will not be completed until next year after basketball season. Yet all you will talk about is that when the new gym is completed, we will be able to practice any time we want to. Participation in the girls' program is at an all-time low. Parents simply find it too difficult to get their children ready for school at 4:30 a.m. It really should not matter that the boys' coach, Coach Nepitino, is the brother-in-law of the superintendent. Think about what we are teaching our young ladies about the role of women in society and the value of women's athletics. Think about the young women who would desperately like to play basketball but are unable because they are unable to attend practice. I could go on but I fear it would do no good.

I am giving you one last chance. If you have not notified me in writing within one week of this e-mail of a change in the gym schedule that provides for equal access for boys' and girls' athletic programs, I will do the following:

1. Immediately resign my teaching and coaching positions at Tightrim Middle School.
2. Send an official letter of complaint to the State Board of Education, the State Standards Commission, the State Middle School Athletic Association, and the Superintendent.
3. I will organize a petition drive demanding your removal from the principalship.
4. I will file a lawsuit alleging discrimination against women at Tightrim Middle School.
5. I will organize the many willing parents who will picket outside of all the boys' basketball games.
6. I will send Op/Ed letters to all of the local newspapers.
7. I will contact and inform all of the local television stations.

I sincerely hope that you will see the justice in my request. If not, you only have yourself to blame.

Sincerely,
Shiny Earlyriser

Prompts:

1. How does this letter impact the dismissal process?
2. What are some implications for leadership presented in this case?
3. What will you do in response to this situation?

Chapter 11

Recent Innovations and Human Resources

INTRODUCTION

A recent article, "4 unusual perks for teachers that districts are trying out" (Education Week Staff, 2019), shared that school districts across the United States are trying out numerous perks to attract and retain teaching staff. Keeping with this theme, this book concludes with a chapter on some unique perks school districts are offering to attract and retain teachers from childcare to housing. This final chapter presents recent innovations in HRD practices in the PreK-12 setting.

More specifically, the chapter includes some innovative perks that districts around the country are implementing in an effort to both attract and retain teachers. Although not all districts will have the means to offer all the perks described, the aim is to provide school leaders suggestions for how they might start reflecting on creative and innovative ways that they might use to attract and retain teachers. In addition, many of the ideas presented reflect emerging trends involving perks offered by school districts across the nation. Following this, the chapter concludes with a summary tying all of the elements of effective HRD at the school level into a guiding framework for effective practice.

RECENT INNOVATIONS

Finding affordable *childcare* is a challenge for most parents. A district in the state of Illinois (Education Week Staff, 2019) recently started offering childcare for their employees and their children aged one month to five years old. This has allowed the district to retain teachers who have recently become new parents and recruit new teaching staff by offering this unique perk. Childcare is expensive and may require a substantial percentage of a teacher's income. This program allows teachers to keep the money from their paycheck and provides the mental well-being and peace of mind that comes with knowing that their child is located on their campus or nearby.

Along with assisting with childcare, some districts also provide *free gym and convenient routine health care* for teachers. This is a longtime practice offered in the business setting by large companies. A school district in the state of Tennessee (Education Week Staff, 2019) now offers a free gym and exercise classes for their staff. In addition to free access to the gym and exercise classes (offered outside of school hours and during lunch hours), they offer a clinic in which there is little or no copay, and a majority of prescriptions are free. This perk has cut down on the number of sick days used by their employees helping the district to cover the cost of the services. Other districts are providing *housing* for teachers.

A district in the state of Arizona (Education Week Staff, 2019) has decided to take on the housing crisis for educators by building a community of tiny, affordable homes in a housing project within the school district boundaries. The district invested $250,000 to build twenty-four homes in a housing community specifically for teachers. This project was completed after the district determined that there were no options for teachers in the form of apartments to rent within the district. Thus, the district decided to be proactive with the thought in mind that their new teachers simply could not afford to purchase a home with their teaching salary.

A district in New York (Education Week Staff, 2019) is offering *paid sabbaticals for K-12 educators* with more than twenty years of service to the district. While paid sabbaticals are prevalent in the higher education setting for professors, this district implemented the practice at the K-12 level. Applications for the sabbatical are reviewed on an annual basis and approved by a review committee. If approved, teachers receive 60 percent of their salary and full benefits during their sabbatical as well as the opportunity to visit other classrooms, other schools, and other school districts. In addition, when teachers return from sabbatical, they are given the opportunity to present and lead professional development in the area(s) they studied during their sabbatical, thus, allowing the sabbatical experience to be beneficial for the entire teaching staff.

In addition to the four perks presented by *Education Week*, there are additional perks being offered by school districts throughout the country. Ideally, districts should aim to offer as many perks as possible. In the examples of perks highlighted thus far, each of the perks was offered by a single school district. Following are cases of school districts offering a variety of perks as a way to recruit and retain teachers (Harrington, 2018).

For example, in the San Francisco Bay Area, one school district has decided to increase teacher salary, provide more training, lower class sizes, alter maternity/parental leave policies, increase common planning time, and develop new housing for their teachers. Quite simply, in an effort to more effectively recruit and retain teaching staff, they decided that implementing multiple perks would be the best approach. These perks are highlighted in greater detail to provide a model for a comprehensive school or district package of incentives to attract and retain teachers. First, there was an *increase in teacher salary*. The pay raises include a $37 million increase in the salary budget for all employees (including nonteaching staff such as administrators, secretaries, and bus drivers) over three years.

This placed the district at the top of their county for teacher pay. This allowed the district to advertise their higher level of pay to both recruit and retain teachers. In addition to the increased pay, the district moved to offer four days of *intensive training for all new teachers* before a given school year begins. This investment in new teachers aimed to show teachers that the district values them and is willing to spend the time and training necessary to orient them to the district. In a majority of school districts, at most, one day is spent on orientation for new hires.

By extending the initial orientation process to four days of intensive training, the district has set the precedent that they value their new teachers and want to ensure that they are ready for the upcoming school year. The increased in-depth training is designed to better prepare new teachers for the rigors of the upcoming academic school year. This training was also initiated to improve the culture in the district's schools as well. *Smaller class sizes* were another component of the district's plan. Going against current trends in the PreK-12 educational setting, the district took a stance on ensuring that class sizes remained reasonable. Many benefits come with smaller class sizes and this is a strong perk for teachers considering coming to the district and retaining teachers who may feel overwhelmed by large classes in the district.

Another unique aspect and important element of the San Francisco model is *maternity/parental leave*. By offering a more generous maternity/parental leave program for employees, the district has set itself apart from other nearby districts, further allowing them to successfully recruit the top teaching prospects in the Bay Area. To further improve the work environment, *increased common planning time* was provided. Paid collaborative planning time for teachers ensures that they have ample time to work together in order to develop lesson, collaborative teaching, and mutual support. Teachers are given the necessary time during the school day to collaborate with their colleagues, which not only improves practice but also fosters relationships among the teaching staff. This paid common planning time includes monthly meetings and two one-day workshops throughout the school year.

Another perk the district planned was to offer affordable housing. The district found that 70 percent of staff who were currently renting had considered leaving the district due to the high cost of housing in the Bay Area, while the same district survey showed 62 percent were interested in living in district-owned rentals. The district offered the apartments at rental rates far below current rent levels in the area. The district made this perk a key initiative after determining that of the renters in their survey, 51 percent paid more than 35 percent of their income for rent and another 12 percent paid a staggering 55 percent of their income for rent.

Although a school may not be able to implement all of the strategies shared in this chapter, there are certainly things all schools and districts can do. The goal is to: "do what you can, with what you have, from where you are." Remember, even the smallest of perks may be the difference between a teacher choosing to work at one school rather than another. Likewise, a school leader should exercise some political sensibility with regard to conversations with principals and other district employees and school board in order to garner support (in some cases financial support) to promote the potential desired in a school or district.

In the San Francisco School District, the leaders did an excellent job of collecting and analyzing data to reinforce the need for the numerous perks to be implemented. Thus, it is wise to first collect data via surveys to determine what perks your current employees recommend and how potential perks might be prioritized and paid for. In the first year, maybe one new perk is offered. In the next year, perhaps another, and so forth. If you have the data that supports the need and benefits of the perks, then you will have the necessary evidence to approve and implement them going forward. In the end, whatever perks are offered, they will likely facilitate more effective recruitment and retention of your teaching staff, and this is critical in attaining the goal of improved teacher quality in a school or district.

Case Reflection 11

"I Want Money, That's What I Want . . ."

It is your fifth year serving as HR director within your district. In analyzing the trend data over the past five years, you have identified that one of the main issues you are facing is retaining your teaching staff. In fact, of the new hires you have personally hired in the past five years, you realize that over 75 percent of them have already left the district. It is apparent that the district must implement some sort of strategy to help retain the teaching staff hired year-to-year. Heeding the advice given in chapter 11 of *Human Resources for School Leaders*, you first want to create a survey and collect additional data before working with your district administrative team to brainstorm possible solutions to your problem. Realizing that this problem not only exists in your district, you have also decided that it might be worthwhile to see what other districts (both nearby and afar) are doing to help combat the problem. Finally, in essence, you want to leave no stone unturned in identifying potential perks you could offer as well as what perks are currently being offered by other school districts. Being mindful of this, and given the information presented in this case reflection, and within the chapter, please answer the following questions.

Questions:

1. Please list in detail what steps you plan to take in order to initiate the process of collecting the necessary data required to determine why teachers are leaving in addition to what would possibly encourage them to stay.
2. After collecting and analyzing the data as part of question 1, the next step is to carefully decide what (if any) perks might be available for you to offer within your district. Hypothetically, share what the data say, and furthermore, what perks you might offer to help retain teachers in your district.
3. In reading chapter 11, numerous perks were shared with regard to what districts across our nation are doing to better recruit and retain teaching staff. Based on your current school setting, choose at least one of the perks shared within this chapter that you believe would be most beneficial to your current school district and why. In sharing this information, explain why you believe it would work and, furthermore, share any potential barriers you see to getting this perk implemented in your district.
4. In addition to the perks shared within chapter 11, what other perks do you believe would be beneficial not only to your school district but also to the teaching profession as a whole? That is, based on your experiences in the PreK-12 educational setting, what other perks might be beneficial in recruiting and retaining teaching staff?
5. Building on question 4, write a general draft of the policy and procedures for implementing at least one of the perks you presented in your response to question 4. In essence, what does this perk look like with regard to the policy and procedures that you would potentially share with district office-level administrators, the school board, and all stakeholders, including students, staff, parents, community members, and business owners?

CONCLUSION

While this book is full of recommendations for school-level leaders to improve the culture and systems related to the relationship between the school organization and the teachers, the fundamental takeaway is the opportunity for school leaders to take a strategic HRD approach to improve teacher quality. This book presents an integrated approach to school-based HRD that aligns culture-building, resource allocation, planning, school policies, leadership practice, operational systems, teacher recruiting, teacher hiring, new teacher induction, and the assessment and development of teachers. As stated in the beginning, this book does not present ideas for increasing teacher quality separate from normal school-based administrative practice; rather, it defines normal practice.

The first section of the book outlines key foundational variables for effective HRD. To begin, the *culture* of a school is the most important factor for successful HRD. A strong culture will attract and retain quality teachers and provide a context for personal growth and improvement. Because it is teachers who actually provide the service schools are created for, the success of any policies, procedures, systems, programs, or initiatives a school implements always depends on the quality, motivation, and behaviors of the professional teachers. An efficient system supported by a strong culture will likely achieve success, and no system is likely to achieve success in a school with toxic culture.

This is the reason for the focus on culture. This said, school-level *leadership* has a profound influence on the culture in a school, especially in regard to the manner in which leaders manage the relationship between the school and its teachers. Roughly 80 percent of the school expenditures are used for teacher salaries and HRD functions. The bulk of this is for teachers' pay. The relative value of this commitment makes HRD an *economic* function. In addition to the fact that when hiring teachers, schools are purchasing services from professional providers, the salaries paid to teachers purchase a finite amount of time. Thus, all decisions regarding how teachers spend professional time has a literal monetary cost and opportunity cost. Because the time of teachers is limited, all decisions regarding the use of the time spend available resources which could be used for other beneficial activities.

Thus, this book places a heavy emphasis throughout on *planning*. SHRP is a process to obtain maximum productivity out of available resources. It is a tool to determine whether decisions regarding the use of time and other resources will result in the most benefit for children, the most learning! The planning chapter (chapter 3) in this book outlines and provides a systematic process for determining the current state of the school, identifying realistic and measureable goals, and developing reasonable actions to obtain the goals. Chapter 4 includes a variety of suggestions for how technology, and ever-increasing and vital tool in the education profession, may be used to support the key foundations of HRD: culture, leadership, economic decision-making, and planning.

The next two sections of the book focus on the utilization of direct HRD process to improve teaching learning. A school can improve teacher quality in two ways. First, a school can replace departing teachers with a teacher who performs at a higher level and/or a school can develop the teaching skills of existing teachers. Section II focuses on the first part and section III focuses on the second.

Schools can and do spend a high level of time and resources on recruiting, hiring, and inducting teachers. The book presents an argument that these are worth a high level of investment because effective hiring and induction reduces the need for future expenditures for hiring and induction. As in all areas of HRD, planning is crucial for obtaining high-quality replacement for departing teachers. It all begins with recruiting, and encouraging quality applicants to apply for teaching positions requires several things. First, principals or HR directors need to have an understanding of the teacher labor market in the region around the school.

Decisions about where and how to target the marketing/recruiting for teachers are critical. Understanding how to brand and present a school to potential applicants is another key to success. Chapter 5 provides a template for clear and concise job description that includes all relevant information and ideas for promoting a school as an attractive place to work. A key caveat is the acknowledgment of the difficulty of selling a school as a good place to work when a school is not a good place to work. This places the onus on the school leadership team to ensure a quality experience for everyone in the school. The next two chapters on hiring and induction continue the focus on planning, assessment, and collaboration.

The hiring process presented in chapter 6 focuses on a collaborative system designed to engage a variety of stakeholders. In addition, multiple suggestions are provided for how to collect and analyze a variety of data to assess the teaching quality and fit of each applicant. A heavy emphasis is placed on the interview and suggestions provided for preparing the interview committee and the need for a focus on how to conduct interviews in a manner that makes the best applicants want to choose the school. Chapter 7 on new teacher induction begins by establishing the goals of new teacher induction as the retention and growth of new teachers. Most importantly, the biggest factor in both growth and retention is not an element of a system; rather, it is the culture of the school that new teachers experience. Regardless, the chapter presents a set of best practices in new teacher induction combined in a comprehensive model. Granted, this model represents an expensive ideal; however, the question school leaders need to consider is: what are the benefits of hiring, retaining, and growing outstanding teachers?

Section III consists of three chapters all focused on linking teacher assessment to professional growth. Professional learning communities are presented as a description of the type of culture consistent with continuous improvement, emphasizing the use of process (primarily qualitative) and output (primarily quantitative) data to support a cycle of assessment, feedback/revisions, growth activity, performance/teaching and then back to assessment. Most importantly, this is a collaborative assessment and learning activity engaged by a community of professionals dedicated to improving,

Once again, success in these areas requires a strong culture, specifically a culture of trust and shared practice. In addition, there is no area where planning is more valuable. The biggest hindrance to effective PLCs, other than a poor culture, is the lack of time. Much time is needed for teachers to share and assess their own practice and the practice of colleagues and continually collaborate to improve. This is the most difficult challenge for school leaders—a challenge this book does not attempt to resolve. This book does posit, in the end, there is no more important benefit a school may commit precious resources toward.

Afterword by Dr. Christopher Colwell

The study of HR as integral for school leader preparation and effectiveness is certainly not new. Every educational leadership degree program teaches HR and every state licensing authority assesses leadership candidate competency in this area. Where Davis and Fowler make a significant contribution to this important topic is in their systemic approach to the role that HR play in every aspect of teaching, learning, and building HR systems in schools that support and sustain academic excellence.

This focus on a systems approach to HRD is of particular value to current practitioners and those who train the next generation of school leaders. Today's school leaders operate in what Bennet and Lemoine (2014) describe as a VUCA environment. That is, an environment that is Volatile, Uncertain, Complex, and Ambiguous. It is not hard to identify each of these VUCA elements in play in today's twenty-first-century school.

All solutions that work in VUCA environments, regardless of the field, require a systems response. The education sector is no different. Leaders who silo the many different aspects of their work as discrete activities or missions to accomplish tend to fail. In short, improving teacher quality does not work in isolation. Davis and Fowler recognize the importance of a comprehensive approach to developing HR that includes a focus on the overall culture of the organization and the many systems that make that culture function successfully.

Human Resources for School Leaders incorporates systems thinking as integral to the success of professional development and overall school performance that are traditionally not connected with HR leadership preparation. The innovative use of technology to improve the myriad aspects and impacts of high-quality HRD and the use of data focused on HR decision-making are two noteworthy examples of this systems approach to HR, all built on a continuous improvement framework.

The authors focus on moving all of these systems much closer to the building level is also an important contribution to the field. It is a common practice to centralize all of the aspects of HR at the district level. From teacher recruiting and hiring to teacher professional development and evaluation, the traditional model of centralized command and control is not the most effective model for meeting the individual needs of each school or for taking advantage of the leadership talent that is spread throughout the school system.

In an environment where the education sector suffers from chronic teacher shortages (Betancourt, 2018), as well as a declining number of current teachers remaining in the profession (Sutcher, Darling-Hammond, & Carver-Thomas, 2016), the need for a robust and comprehensive approach for improving the capacity of teachers, and just as importantly, the satisfaction of teachers with the climate and culture of the schools in which they work has never been more important. *Human Resources for School Leaders* succeeds in developing a comprehensive, systems approach to the importance, and impact, of human capital and school leadership.

Dr. Chris Colwell
Stetson University

References

American Recovery and Reinvestment Act of 2009. P.L. 111–115.
Arghode, V., Brieger, E. W., & McLean, G. N. (2017). Adult learning theories: Implications for online instruction. *European Journal of Training and Development, 41*(7), 593–609. doi:10.1108/EJTD-02-2017-0014
Bandura, A. (1997). *Self-efficacy: The exercise of control.* New York: W.H. Freeman.
Barnes, G. M., Crowe, E., & Schaefer, B. (2007). *The cost of teacher turnover in five school districts: A pilot study.* Washington, DC: National Commission on Teaching and America's Future.
Bennett, N., & Lemoine, J. (2014). What VUCA really means for you. *Harvard Business Review, 92*(1,2), 27.
Betancourt, S. (2018, Sept. 8). Teacher shortages are worsening in most states. *The Guardian.* Retrieved at https://www.theguardian.com/us-news/2018/sep/06/teacher-shortages-guardian-survey-schools
Blankstein, A. (2013). *Failure is not an option: 6 principles that advance student achievement in highly effective schools* (3rd ed.). New York: Corwin.
Borman, G. D., & Dowling, N. M. (2008). Teacher attrition and retention: A meta-analytic and narrative review of the research. *Review of Educational Research, 78*(3), 367–409.
Bridges, E. M. (1992). *The incompetent teacher: Managerial responses.* Washington, DC: Falmer Press.
Bubb, S., Earley, P., & Totterdell, M. (2005). Accountability and responsibility: "Rogue" school leaders and the induction of new teachers in England. *Oxford Review of Education, 31,* 255–272. doi:10.1080/03054980500117884
Burnham, T. (Oct. 2019). Personal communication.
Carver-Thomas, D., & Darling-Hammond, L. (2017). *Teacher turnover: Why it matters and what we can do about it.* Palo Alto, CA: Learning Policy Institute.
Carver-Thomas, D., & Darling-Hammond, L. (2019). The trouble with teacher turnover: How teacher attrition affects students and schools. *Education Policy Analysis Archives, 27*(36), 36. doi:10.14507/epaa.27.3699

References

Casas, J. (2018). *Thought for the day, March 16, 2018*. Retrieved from: https://twitter.com/casas_jimmy/status/974666039110795264

Cavanagh, S. (2017). K-12 spending: Where the money goes. *Ed Week Market Brief*, June 1, 2017. Retrieved from: https://marketbrief.edweek.org/marketplace-k-12/k-12-spending-where-the-money-goes/

Dangel, J. R. (Ed.) (2006). *Research on teacher induction*. Lanham, MD: Rowman & Littlefield Education.

Davis, D. R., Ellett, C. D., & Annunziata, J. (2002). Teacher evaluation, leadership and learning organizations. *Journal of Personnel Evaluation in Education, 16*(4), 287–302.

Davis, D. R., Pool, J. E., & Mits-Cash, M. (2000). Issues in implementing a new teacher assessment system in a large school district: Results of a qualitative field study. *Journal of Personnel Evaluation in Education, 14*(4), 285–306.

Deming, W. E. (1986). *Out of the crisis*. Cambridge: Massachusetts Institute of Technology, Center for Advanced Engineering Study.

Dewey, J. (1919). *Democracy and education: An introduction to the philosophy of education*. New York: Macmillan company.

Dewey, J. (1938). *Experience and education*. New York: Macmillan Company.

Duke, D. L., (1990). Developing teacher evaluation systems that promote professional growth. *Journal of Personnel Evaluation in Education, 4*(2), 131–144.

Edmonds, R. R. (1981). Making public schools effective. *Social Policy, 12*(2), 56–60.

Edmonds, R. R. (1982). Programs of school improvement: An overview. *Educational Leadership, 40*(3), 4–11.

Education Week Staff. (2019). 4 unusual perks for teachers that districts are trying out. *Education Week*. Retrieved from: https://www.edweek.org/ew/articles/2019/03/01/4-unusual-perks-for-teachers-that-districts.html

Educational Research Service. (1988). *Teacher evaluation: Practices and procedures*. Arlington, VA: Author.

Ellett, C. D., & Garland, J. (1987). Teacher evaluation practices in our largest school districts: Are they measuring up to "state-of-the-art" systems? *Journal of Personnel Evaluation in Education, 1*(1), 69–92.

Elmore, R. F. (2000). *Building a new structure for school leadership*. Washington, DC: Albert Shanker Institute.

Elmore, R. F. (2016). "Getting to scale . . ." it seemed like a good idea at the time. *Journal of Educational Change, 17*(4), 529–537. doi:10.1007/s10833-016-9290-8

Engel, M., Jacob, B. A., & Curran, F. C. (2014). New evidence on teacher labor supply. *American Educational Research Journal, 51*(1), 36–72. doi:10.3102/0002831213503031

Follett, M. P. (1919). Community is a process. *Philosophical Review, 28*, 576–588.

Fullan, M. (2001). *Leading in a culture of change*. San Francisco, CA: Jossey-Bass.

Fullen, M. (2015). *The new meaning of educational change*, (5th ed.) New York, NY: Teachers College Press.

Fullan, M., & Quinn, J. (2016). *Coherence: The right drivers in action for schools, districts, and systems*. Thousand Oaks, CA: Corwin.

Fullan, M., Hill, P., & Crevola, C. (2006). *Breakthrough*. Thousand Oaks, CA: Sage.

Glossary of Education Reform. (n.d.). Retrieved from: https://www.edglossary.org/school-culture/

Goddard, R., Goddard, Y., Kim, E. S., & Miller, R. (2015). A theoretical and empirical analysis of the roles of instructional leadership, teacher collaboration, and collective efficacy beliefs in support of student learning. *American Journal of Education*, *121*(4), 501–530.

Goldstein, D. (2014). *The teacher wars: A history of America's most embattled profession* (1st ed.). New York: Doubleday.

Guarino, C. M., Santibañez, L., & Daley, G. A. (2006). Teacher recruitment and retention: A review of the recent empirical literature. *Review of Educational Research*, *76*(2), 173–208. doi:10.3102/00346543076002173

Gullickson, A. (2008). *The personnel evaluation standards: How to assess systems for evaluating educators* (2nd ed.). Thousand Oaks, CA: Corwin.

Hallinger, P., & Heck, R. H. (1998). Exploring the principal's contribution to school effectiveness: 1980–1995. *School Effectiveness and School Improvement: An International Journal of Research, Policy and Practice*, *9*, 157–191. http://dx.doi.org/10.1080/0924345980090203

Hallinger, P., & Murphy, J. F. (1986). The social context of effective schools. *American Journal of Education*, *94*(3), 328.

Hanushek, E. A. (2011). The economic value of higher teacher quality. *Economics of Education Review*, *30*(3), 466–479. doi:10.1016/j.econedurev.2010.12.006

Harrington, T. (2018). *Higher pay, smaller classes, housing perks in San Francisco Bay Area district's plan to attract teachers*. EdSource. Retrieved from: https://edsource.org/2018/more-pay-smaller-classes-housing-perks-in-bay-area-districts-plan-to-lure-california-teachers/599896

Heilbronn, R. (2017). Dewey and culture: Responding to "Extreme views." *Journal of Philosophy of Education*, *51*(1), 89–101. doi:10.1111/1467-9752.12217

Heneman, H. G., & Milanowski, A. T. (2003). Continuing assessment of teacher reactions to a standards-based teacher evaluation system. *Journal of Personnel Evaluation in Education*, *17*(1), 173–195. https://doi.org/10.1023/B:PEEV.0000032427.99952.02

Hoy, W. K., & Miskel, C. G. (2013). *Educational administration: Theory, research, and practice* (9th ed.). New York: McGraw Hill.

Ingersoll, R. M., & Strong, M. (2011). The impact of induction and mentoring programs for beginning teachers: A critical review of the research. *Review of Educational Research*, *81*(2), 201–233. doi:10.3102/0034654311403323

Ingersoll, R., Merrill, L., & Stuckey, D. (2014). *Seven trends: The transformation of the teaching force* (Updated April 2014). Consortium for Policy Research in education. Retrieved from: https://cpre.org/sites/default/files/workingpapers/1506_7trendsapril2014.pdf

Jackson Public Schools. (2018). Excellence for all: The strategic plan for educating Jackson scholars, 2019–2024. Retrieved from: https://www.jackson.k12.ms.us/domain/4497

Jehangir, K., Glas, C. A. W., & van den Berg, S. (2015). Exploring the relation between socio-economic status and reading achievement in PISA 2009 through an intercepts-and-slopes-as-outcomes paradigm. *International Journal of Educational Research, 71,* 1–15. doi:10.1016/j.ijer.2015.02.002

Knouse, S., Carson, P., Carson, K., & Heady, R. (2009). Improve constantly and forever. *The TQM Journal, 21*(5), 449–461. doi:10.1108/17542730910983371

Kozan, K. (2019). *Diversity hiring: 6 steps to hiring more diverse candidates.* Ideal. Retrieved from: https://ideal.com/diversity-hiring/

Kurland, H., Peretz, H., & Hertz-Lazarowitz, R. (2010). Leadership style and organizational learning: The mediate effect of school vision. *Journal of Educational Administration, 48*(1), 7–30. Retrieved from: https://doi.org/10.1108/09578231011015395

Loup, K. S., Garland, J. S., Ellett, C. D., & Rugutt, J. K. (1996). Ten years later: Findings from a replication of a study of teacher evaluation practices in our 100 largest school districts. *Journal of Personnel Evaluation in Education, 10,* 203–226.

Malik, M. (2016). Assessment of a professional development program on adult learning theory. *Portal: Libraries and the Academy, 16*(1), 47–70. doi:10.1353/pla.2016.0007

Marzano, R. J., Waters, T., & McNulty, B. A. (2005). *School leadership that works: From research to results.* Alexandria, VA: Association for Supervision and Curriculum Development.

McCarthy, N. (2019, April 2). The evolution of U.S. teacher salaries in the 21st century. *Forbes.* Retrieved at https://www.forbes.com/sites/niallmccarthy/2019/04/02/the-evolution-of-u-s-teacher-salaries-in-the-21st-century-infographic/#6762e1b277f0

McQueen, D., & Burnham, T. (2015). *Guidelines to strategic planning.* Unpublished manuscript.

Mississippi Department of Education. (2019). Retrieved from: https://www.mdek12.org/OPR/Reporting/Accountability/2019

Nataf, E. (2018). *Educational technology in 2018.* Teacher Gaming. Retrieved from: https://store.teachergaming.com/blog/educational-technology-in-2018-n29

National Association of College Employees. (n.d.). Retrieved from: https://www.naceweb.org

No Child Left Behind Act of 2001, P.L. 107–110, 20 U.S.C. § 6319 (2002).

Peterson, K. D. (1995). *Teacher evaluation: A comprehensive guide to new directions and practices.* Thousand Oaks, CA: Corwin Press.

Printy, S. M., & Marks, H. M. (2006). Shared leadership for teacher and student learning. *Theory Into Practice, 45*(2), 125–132.

Ross, J. A., & Gray, P. (2006). Transformational leadership and teacher commitment to organizational values: The mediating effects of collective teacher efficacy. *School Effectiveness and School Improvement, 17*(2), 179–199.

Schuette v Coalition to Defend Affirmative Action, 134 S. Ct. 1623, 1667 (2014).

Scriven, M. (1990). Teacher selection. In Millman, J., & Darling-Hammond, L. *The new handbook of teacher evaluation* (pp. 77–103). London: SAGE Publications Ltd. doi: 10.4135/9781412986250

Smith, A. (2015). *U.S. smartphone use in 2015.* Pew Research Center. Retrieved from: https://www.pewresearch.org/internet/2015/04/01/us-smartphone-use-in-2015/

Smith, T. M., & Ingersoll, R. M. (2004). What are the effects of induction and mentoring on beginning teacher turnover? *American Educational Research Journal, 41*(3), 681–714. doi:10.3102/00028312041003681

Smith, W., & Ellett, C. D. (2000). *Reconceptualizing school leadership for the 21st century: Music, metaphors, and leadership density*. Paper presented at the Annual Meeting of the American Educational Research Association (New Orleans, Louisiana, April 24–28, 2000). Retrieved from: https://eric.ed.gov/?id=ED468511

Snyder, T. D., de Brey, C., & Dillow, S. A. (2019). *Digest for education statistics, 2017* (53rd ed.). Washington, DC: National Center for Education Statistics. Retrieved from: https://nces.ed.gov/pubs2018/2018070.pdf

Stiggins, R. J., & Duke, D. L. (1988). *The case for commitment to teacher growth: Research on teacher evaluation*. Albany, NY: State University of New York Press.

Stout, M., & Love, J. M. (2015). *Integrative process: Follettian thinking from ontology to administration*. Anoka, MN: Process Century Press.

Sutcher, L., Darling-Hammond, L., & Carver-Thomas, D. (2016). *A coming crises in teaching? Teacher supply, demand, and shortages in the U.S.* Palo Alto, CA: Learning Policy Institute.

Švarc, J. (2016). The knowledge worker is dead: What about professions? *Current Sociology, 64*(3), 392–410. Retrieved from: https://doi.org/10.1177/0011392115591611

Tate, E. (2019). #SuperintendentsSoWhite: Three takeaways from the annual survey of school leaders. *EdSurge*, February 19, 2019. Retrieved from: https://www.edsurge.com/news/2019-02-19-superintendentssowhite-three-takeaways-from-the-annual-survey-of-school-leaders

Teddlie, C., Kirby, P. C., & Stringfield, S. (1989). Effective versus ineffective schools: Observable differences in the classroom. *American Journal of Education, 97*(3), 221–236.

Tucker, P. D. (1997). Lake Wobegon: Where all teachers are competent (or, have we come to terms with the problem of incompetent teachers?). *Journal of Personnel Evaluation in Education, 11*, 103–126.

Ungarino, R. (2015). *For more poor Americans, smartphones are lifelines*. CNBC. Retrieved from: http://www.cnbc.com/2015/04/01/for-more-poor-americans-smartphones-are-lifelines.html

Upper Arlington Schools. (2018). *Quality profile report*. Upper Arlington District Website. Retrieved from: https://www.uaschools.org/Downloads/quality%20profile%2017- 18%20FINAL.pdf

U.S. Constitution, Amendment X.

von Stumm, S. (2017). Socioeconomic status amplifies the achievement gap throughout compulsory education independent of intelligence. *Intelligence, 60*, 57–62. doi:10.1016/j.intell.2016.11.006

von Stumm, S., & Plomin, R. (2015). Socioeconomic status and the growth of intelligence from infancy through adolescence. *Intelligence, 48*, 30–36. doi:10.1016/j.intell.2014.10.002

von Stumm, S., Deary, I. J., & Hagger-Johnson, G. (2013). Life-course pathways to psychological distress: A cohort study. *BMJ Open, 3*(5), e002772. doi:10.1136/bmjopen-2013-002772

Whipps, J. (2014). A pragmatist reading of Mary Parker Follett's integrative process. *Transactions of the Charles S. Peirce Society: A Quarterly Journal in American Philosophy, 50*(3), 405–424. doi:10.2979/trancharpeirsoc.50.3.405

Wright, S. P., Horn, S. P., & Sanders, W. L. (1997). Teacher and classroom context effects on student achievement: Implications for teacher evaluation. *Journal of Personnel Evaluation in Education, 11*(1), 57–67.

Young, R. (2017). Personal communication.

Zepeda, S. J., & Ponticell, J. A. (1998). At cross-purposes: What do teachers need, want, from supervision? *Journal of Curriculum and Supervision, 14*(1), 68–87.

About the Authors

Dr. Douglas R. Davis is an associate professor and the director of doctoral programs in K-12 Leadership at the University of Mississippi. He earned a BS in history at Southern Oregon College, a BS in secondary social studies education at Oregon State University, and an MEd and PhD in education administration and supervision from Louisiana State University. While attending graduate school, he taught high school social studies and coached football and wrestling in the Baton Rouge area for seven years. His dissertation, an oral history of the experience of teachers during the "crossover" transition of faculty during desegregation just prior to the 1970 school year, remains one of the only studies to document the meaning teachers ascribed to their experiences as teachers during desegregation. Following earning his doctorate, he spent seven years on the faculty at Georgia State University where he coordinated the MEd, EdS, and PhD programs in K-12 Leadership. In, 2007, he took a position as an associate professor of K-12 Leadership at the University of Mississippi where he has coordinated the K-12 Leadership programs and is now serving as director of doctoral programs. During his tenure as a professor, he has served as the editor of the *Journal of Personnel Evaluation in Education* (now the *Journal of Educational Assessment, Evaluation, and Accountability*), the *Journal of Thought*, president of the Consortium for Research on Educational Assessment and Teacher Evaluation (CREATE), and president of the Society of History and Philosophy of Education (SOPHE). He recently led the design of a Carnegie Program on the Educational Doctorate EdD program at the University of Mississippi that is now entering its fifth year. He has chaired over thirty doctoral dissertations. In addition, he has a commitment to issues of sustainability and education, including student well-being and health issues, especially in regard to healthy diet. In this area and with a commitment to sustainability, he started one of the first organic community supported agriculture farms in north Mississippi: Yokna Bottoms Farm is now in its tenth season. He has been active in Good Food for Oxford Schools, the Mississippi Farm to School Network, the Mississippi Sustainable Agriculture Network, and the Oxford Community Market, where he is currently the chair of the Board of Directors.

Dr. Denver J. Fowler is an internationally acclaimed higher education leader, professor, author, speaker, researcher, and former practitioner in the field of PK-12 educational leadership. Based in the United States, Dr. Fowler currently serves as an Associate Professor of Educational Leadership and Policy Studies at Southern Connecticut State University in New Haven,

Connecticut. Prior to this appointment, he served as an Interim Chair of the School of Education, the Chair of the Doctor of Education (Ed.D.) program, and Professor of PK-12 Educational Leadership at Franklin University. Prior to his appointment at Franklin University, spanning a decade, Dr. Fowler held appointments at The Ohio State University, The University of Mississippi, Bowling Green State University, California State University-Sacramento, and University of West Florida, respectively. In addition, he served for over a decade in the PK-12 educational setting as a coach, teacher, athletic director, technology coordinator, and school administrator. Dr. Fowler has numerous publications in the form of peer-reviewed journals and chapters, articles in top practitioner magazines, and books on the topic of educational leadership. His most recent book titled *The 21st Century School Leader: Leading Schools in Today's World* consistently remains a best-seller amongst both practitioners in the field and colleges/universities preparing aspiring school leaders, including principals and superintendents. Dr. Fowler also serves as the Associate Editor for the *Journal of Research in Innovative Teaching & Learning*, and continuously serves a peer-reviewer for numerous journals and conferences. A renowned researcher on the topic of ethics and school leadership, he has presented his research both nationally and internationally, including presentations in China, Greece, Japan, Italy, Turkey, England, Puerto Rico, Spain, and Africa. A proud scholar-practitioner, Dr. Fowler is an award-winning school administrator, and was once named the Ohio Association of Secondary School Administrators and National Association of Secondary School Principals *Assistant Principal of the Year* (APOY) in the state of Ohio, and nominated for the APOY in the United States. He received this award and nomination for successfully leading a school turn-around initiative in which his school received all A's on their state report card. Dr. Fowler has also received Congressional Recognition from the United States House of Representatives for his dedication and service to the PK-12 educational setting. A strong advocate for educational policy reform, Dr. Fowler has spoken on Capitol Hill representing our nation's school leaders, educators and students, advocating for Bills that would benefit our nation's lowest performing schools. Dr. Fowler completed his Doctor of Education (Ed.D.) at Ohio University, Master of Arts in Education (M.A.) at Mount Vernon Nazarene University, Bachelor of Science in Education (B.S.) at The Ohio State University, and completed a School Leadership Institute at Harvard University. A lifelong learner, he is currently enrolled in the Graduate Certificate in Educational Law program at Indiana University. To this day, he remains a licensed Superintendent, Principal, and Teacher (in numerous U.S. states), and also holds a private school Administrative and Teaching license.

Index

academic excellence, 133
achievement: academic, 53; disaggregated, 105; gaps, xviii, 92, 105; goals, 6, 105; improving, 92; life, 29; mission and vision, 33; output measures, 98; student, 11, 96, 104–9; teacher impact, 20
adequacy versus excellence, 86, 111
administrative support: districts, xix; teacher retention, 24
applicants: assessing, 18, 61–69; hiring, 28; minority, 50; potential, 47; pre-screening, 65; qualifications, 22, 59, 62, 68, 69; recruiting, 47, 58, 130
apps: Classroom Walkthrough App, 49; Hootsuite App, xv, 52; HRD in, xix
assessment: benchmark, 21; current practice, 94–96; dismissal of teachers, 120; district-level, 97–99; formative, 79, 88; efficiency, 29; hiring, 12, 62–68; large scale, 93–95; leading, 15, 94; mentor training, 78; merit, 62; new teacher needs, 77; organizational needs, 43; performance, 92; planning, 35, 105–7; professional growth, 83–85; school level, 99–102; student, 79; teacher, 43, 85–88, 94; worth, 62

Bandura, Albert: efficacy, 87
building level: HRD, xix, 3, 134; strategic planning, 33, 36; teacher evaluation, 99–102; teacher removal, 119
Burnham, Tom, 36–38

celebrating: Jackson Public Schools, 40; new teachers, 48, 49; through technology, 52
central office: role, xix, 5, 37, 43, 119
coherency, 29
collaboration: evaluation, 117; mentoring, 77, 79; professional growth, 11; stakeholders, 85, 106; teacher, satisfaction, 24; teachers, time, 86
commitment: JPS, 5 Commitments, 43–44; professional growth, 86; teacher dismissal, 115, 117, 119; time, 80
common planning time, 126
communication technology, 46–53
conflict, 6, 15, 60, 116, 117
continuous improvement, xx, 8, 110, 119, 131, 134
core values, 37, 39–40, 77
cost, 5, 20, 21–24, 27–29, 77; cost-benefit analysis, 28; fixed, 29;

induction, 80; marginal teaching, 20, 116; opportunity, 21, 23, 27, 28, 60, 129; professional development, 105, 109; replacing teacher, 31; student per year, 31, 32; teacher evaluation, 98; teacher hiring, 63; teacher recruiting, 58–61; variable, 29

culture: interviews, 69; leadership, and, 15, 16; organizational, xviii, 4, 6, 6–10, 29, 57, 62, 64, 98, 118, 129; planning, 30; professional, 6, 26; professional development, 85; respectful, 40; teacher dismissal, 116; teacher evaluation, 84, 85, 100, 126; teacher induction, 48, 73, 80; teacher leaders, 32; teacher retention, 23; technology, 46, 52, 53

Darling Hammond, Linda, xvii, 134

data: achievement gaps, 92, 108; assessment, 84, 103; attendance, 43; cycle of assessment, 131

decisions, xix, 8, 29, 94; discipline, 42; due process, 119–20; hiring, 62, 67, 68; internal, 34; marginal teachers, 115, 119; observation, 84; output, 105, 107; planning, 35; preliminary screening, 64; process, 107; professional development, 106; qualitative, 30; quantitative, 107

Deming, Edwards, 7–8, 29; 14 points (principles) of quality, 8, 29; continuous improvement, 8; data-based decision making, 29

Dewey, John, 7

digital footprint, 51

district: communication, 52; hiring, 57, 59, 61; labor market, 22, 27, 32; large, 31; local education agency, 5; low SES, 47; perks, 124; personnel policies, 119–20; rural, 23; spending, 19, 124; strategic planning, 36; suburban, 23; teacher evaluation, 95, 97–99

diversity, 7, 11, 46, 49, 50, 62, 63

due process, 119–20
Duke, Daniel, 84–88

economics, xv, xix, 19, 20, 23, 28
effective schools research, 9
efficacy, 11, 84, 87
Ellett, Chad: leadership density and capacity, 3; teacher evaluation, 84, 85, 94–96, 101
Elmore, Richard, 5, 7, 10
ethics: current practices, 16; dilemmas, 118; hiring, 61–63, 69; removing teachers, 116; teacher evaluation, 96; teacher recruiting, 58, 59; trust, 86
evaluation: data, 63, 95, 119; dismissal, 116, 117, 119; district, 97–99; formative, 95, 98; hiring, 67; Personnel Evaluation Standards, 94–97; practices, 28, 84, 88, 94–96, 118, 119; process, 83, 86, 118; professional growth, 104–10; school level, 99–102; summative, 98; systems, 88, 99, 101, 118–19
expectations: committee (charging), 64; high, 40, 43, 87; societal, 115; teaching and learning, 118

Follett, Mary Parker, 7
Fullan, Michael, 7, 9

gap analysis, 34, 105, 107, 108
goals: excellence and adequacy, 86; measurable, 130; organizational, 3, 6, 7, 26, 106, 107; outcome, 107, 109; professional development, 105, 108; purpose, 3; statement, 37; strategic planning, 37, 38, 41–43, 58
goods, 5, 20
Greene, Errick, 39–41
Gross Domestic Product, 20
guidelines: financial, 5; teacher dismissal, 119; teacher recruitment, 58

Hanushek, Eric, xviii
hashtag, 47, 49, 51, 52

Heneman, Herbert, 97–99
hiring: diversity, 50; improvement through, 26, 43; interviews, 47, 48, 63, 64, 67–69, 130; perks, 46, 124–27, 128; processes, 11, 30, 57, 61–70, 96, 129; value, 17, 21, 28, 30, 31
Hoy, Wayne, 5

implementation over instrumentation, 98
incompetent teachers: problems with, 115–19
innovations, 8, 124–27
integrity, 86

Jackson Public Schools: Excellence for All, 39; strategic plan, 38–44
Jazz Combo School, 96
Joint Committee on Personnel Evaluation Standards, 96
JPS. *See* Jackson Public Schools

Knight in Shining Armor, 98

leadership: challenges and opportunities, 12, 15–16; change, 98; culture, 129; definition, 3; density, 3; hiring, 62; HRD, xviii, 3; motivation, 87; organizational, 4; paradox, 4–6; practice, 19, 26, 27; professional development, 105–10; shared instructional, 84; standards, 9; strategic planning, 35; teacher, 32; themes, 4

management, 8, 15, 77
marginal teachers, 21, 78, 115–19
marketing: advertising, 60, 61; branding, 46, 51 130; rebranding, 51; teacher recruiting, 58–61, 130
McQueen, Doug, 36–38
mentoring: cost, 27, 78; culture, 73; fit, 79; impact, 80; quality, 78, 80; support, 27; teaching, as, 78; training, 78; value, 27

merit: ethics, 67, 68; hiring, 50, 61–63
Miami-Dade County Schools, 95, 99
Milanowski, Anthony, 97–99
Miskel, Cecil, 5
mission statement, 33, 34, 36–38, 39, 41, 44, 106
Mississippi, 38

NAEP. *See* National Assessment of Educational Progress
National Assessment of Educational Progress, 38
NCLB. *See* No Child Left Behind
No Child Left Behind, 4, 92

observation, 28, 34, 35, 49, 77–79, 84, 98, 100, 101, 118–20
opportunity cost, 21, 23, 27, 28, 60, 129

PACES. *See* Professional Assessment and Comprehensive Evaluation System
pedagogical practice, 104
performance standards, 94, 108
perks, 46, 47, 124–27
Personnel Evaluation Standards, 94–97; accuracy standard, 96; feasibility standard, 96; joint committee, 96, 97; propriety standard, 96; utility standard, 96
placement offices, 60
PLC. *See* Professional Learning Community
position announcement, 59
poverty rate, 31, 39
preliminary screening, 64
product, 20, 92
production: control, 6; cost, 29; efficiency, 19; factors of, 22; process, as, 92; teaching and learning, as, 19, 31
profession, teaching: behavior, 11; characteristics, 5; culture, 9–10, 26; labor market, 22–24; license, 5;

needs, 21; quality, xviii; quasi, 5; recognition and autonomy, 5; status, xvii
Professional Assessment and Comprehensive Evaluation System (PACES), 96–99
professional development: activities, 105; adult learning, 105; costs, 27, 28, 88; data-based, 107, 109; developing HRD, 104; evaluation for, 85, 94–97, 102; leadership, 105–10; outcome goals, 108; planning, 109, 110; providers, 21; return on investment, 80; *versus* staff development, 85, 86
Professional Learning Community, xviii, 83, 88, 119, 131

qualified teacher, xvii, 23
quality profile report, 52, 53
quasi-profession, 5

Race to the Top, 92
recruiting, 46, 47, 58–61
remediation, 21, 86, 94, 118–20
research, 17, 18
retention, teacher: culture, 40; healthy attrition, 22–24; induction, 11, 27, 30, 43, 73, 79, 80, 129, 130–31; technology, 48
RTT. *See* Race to the Top

sabbaticals, 125
San Francisco School District, 125–27
school board, 5, 22, 36–38, 52, 117, 120, 127
selection committee, 63–65, 67, 68, 70
service, 5, 20
shared instructional leadership, 84
stakeholder: buy-in, 35; collaboration, 30, 33, 36–38, 39, 64, 99, 100, 106, 130; communication, 48, 53; perception, 51, 117
strategic planning, 33–44; core values, 37, 39–40; guidelines, 35, 36; recruiting and hiring teachers, 57
supply, 23, 23, 58
supply and demand, teachers, 22, 23
sustained school improvement, xx

teacher: autonomy and control, 5; capacity, xviii; costs, 21, 27–29, 31, 36; dismissal, 94, 115–20; diversity, 49, 50; hiring, 47–48, 61–70, 124–27; induction, 27, 28, 35, 48, 49, 76–80; labor market, 20–23, 26; marginal, xix–xx, 16, 21, 32, 78, 115, 117, 119; planning, 35; professional, 4; quality, 11, 47; recruiting, 46, 47, 58–61; shortage, 39; value, 19, 27–29
teaching and learning: assessing, 83–88; behavioral process, 7, 11, 84, 119; HRD, 11, 12; induction, 48; production of (service), 19, 32; professional growth, 92–94, 105–10; student engagement, 100
Tenth Amendment, 4
training: 14 points (Deming), 7–8; interviewer, 69; mentor, 28, 77, 78; new teachers, 126; teacher assessor, 16, 95, 98, 100, 101, 112
Tucker, Pamela, 115–17

United Teachers of Miami-Dade County, 95

variability, 118–19
vision: core values, 77; goals, 106; leadership, 15; portrait, 43; school, 32; shared, 6, 9; statement, 33, 36–40

walk-through, 49, 100

www.ingramcontent.com/pod-product-compliance
Lightning Source LLC
Chambersburg PA
CBHW051812230426
43672CB00012B/2710